48 DAYS

TO THE WORK YOU LOVE

DAN MILLER

48 DAYS

TO THE WORK YOU LOVE

B&H
PUBLISHING GROUP

NASHVILLE, TENNESSEE

© 2007 by Dan Miller
All rights reserved
Printed in the United States of America

978-0-8054-4479-7

Published by B & H Publishing Group
Nashville, Tennessee

Dewey Decimal Classification: 248.84
Subject Headings: CHRISTIAN LIFE
                   VOCATIONAL GUIDANCE

Originally published as hard-cover edition: ISBN 0-8054-3188-8

1 2 3 4 5 6 7 8 9 10   11 10 09 08 07

Contents

Foreword

Few categories of our lives define us and grow us spiritually, emotionally, relationally, and as people. Our work is one of those powerful defining areas. Sadly, a j-o-b is what most people settle for, but as Dan Miller so powerfully points out in the coming chapters, a *calling* lights up your life.

Dan's insight and actual hands-on implementation of discovering and developing a calling has influenced thousands of lives, including mine and many of my team members'. You see, implementation is the key. In the last few years I have been very inspired to be "wild at heart" and to have a "purpose-driven life" and am a huge fan of those culture-impacting books (by John Eldredge and Rick Warren, respectively). I am even more excited by *48 Days to the Work You Love* because it puts clothes on the concepts. You may be like me; I sometimes need someone to help me put the concepts into action. Knowledge without action is personified in the overeducated broke and broken who wander listlessly among us.

The following pages lead you to implement a step-by-step plan to show the world your purpose and your heart in a way that is most satisfying. It is satisfying not because you will never face adversity or make mistakes in the process—nor because your career will zoom ahead and never falter. You will fall, you will err, and your career will not take a perfect path. No, this material is satisfying and life-changing because you will have the tools to discover a key part of the plan God has for your life. This material is satisfying because when you begin discovering and *implementing* this plan, you will have a sense of God-given power that will propel you through adversity and errors. This new God-given power will give you the energy to recognize that even wrong turns can benefit the end result.

In the last several years, while meeting and spending time with people who have become inordinately successful, I have observed several common traits among them. Two of those traits stand out. One is they have a calling, which they have discovered and are implementing. The other is they have made mountains of mistakes in the process of becoming "successful." The gleaming mountain of success is actually a pile of trash—a pile of the mistakes we have made. The difference between the successful and the troubled is not error-free living; it is that by discovering and implementing a life calling, the successful stand on their pile of trash while the troubled sit under theirs.

Most of us spend too much of our lives in paralyzing fear, shame, guilt, and dread when it comes to our work. Work has become the daily grind instead of the great adventure it should be. The beauty of this material is that as you implement it, you will gradually process your negative emotions and move into a thriving work life. As someone who lives this material everyday, I know you will still experience doubt, fear, and mistakes. However, by finding and functioning in your calling, you will increasingly grow in confidence that you were put here to win in spite of those things, not without them.

I am excited for you because by opening these next few pages you are lighting a fire. The wood may be old and wet, but it has the capacity to become a raging bonfire! This is a book about implementation, *so do it!*

DAVE RAMSEY
Nationally Syndicated
Radio Host

Introduction

Very early in life we begin to determine what we want to be when we grow up. And as we grow, there is a subtle yet significant transition from "what do I want to *be*?" to "what am I going to *do*?" We are defined and valued in America by what we *do*. Unfortunately, the path to *doing* something often bypasses the basic questions about *being* something.

Webster's dictionary defines *work* as "bodily or mental effort exerted to do or make something; purposeful activity." Interestingly, those who hate their jobs by definition aren't "working" (purposeful activity) because they are doing something they hate. (Maybe we can come up with a new word for people who spend their time doing something they hate: e.g., "Lifebotcher," "Wasteoholic," "Insaniac,"—send me suggestions at dan.miller@48Days.com.) The consumer research center for the Conference Board in New York reports that there may have been sharp declines in many areas of job satisfaction in the American workforce since 1995. Their September 2003 study found that only 50.7 percent of respondents overall said they're satisfied with their current jobs. And that's a downward change of 13.5 percent from 1995, when 58.6 percent of those asked said they were satisfied. For many people, work has become nothing more than a paycheck. It is an accepted stance to hate our jobs and to belittle the boss and the company—even for those attempting to live out God's purpose in their lives.

"I LOATHE MY WORK!"

I hear a lot of poignant phrases from people describing their work. "I loathe my work" came from a Christian attorney during a recent coaching session. According to *Webster's* dictionary, to *loathe* is "to feel intense dislike, disgust, or hatred for; abhor, [or] detest" something. Obviously, it's pretty difficult to put yourself into your work if you loathe it. You could perform as others expect and get a paycheck, but you are not likely to experience meaning, purpose, peace, or fulfillment in work you loathe.

FARM-RAISED

I was raised on a dairy farm in rural Ohio. My father was a farmer and the pastor of the small Mennonite church in our one-caution-light town, which gave me a unique perspective on the world. Fulfilling God's will meant honoring my father and mother, attending church at least 3 times a week, not swearing like my town buddies, and keeping my word. Going to ball games, swimming pools, proms, dances, and having free time was out. Fancy cars, TVs, current fashions, and other "worldly" possessions were absolutely forbidden. Work was a constant, 7-days-a-week activity. Cows needed to be milked twice a day, 365 days a year. Corn needed to be planted, hay needed to be mowed, and chicken coops needed to be cleaned.

I had no freedom to consider what kind of work I wanted to do or was called to do. Any wishes, desires, dreams, or callings were squeezed around the realities of life—work had to be done just to survive. The luxury of "enjoying" work was not discussed. Wasn't work only something we do to pass time through this earthly life until we reach our heavenly reward? Doesn't the Bible tell us that work was the resulting curse to Adam for eating from the tree of life?

"The ground is cursed because of you.
You will eat from it by means of painful labor
all the days of your life.
It will produce thorns and thistles for you,
and you will eat the plants of the field.
You will eat bread by the sweat of your brow
until you return to the ground,

since you were taken from it.
For you are dust,
and you will return to dust." (Gen. 3:17–19)

Now, I understood that "sweat of your brow" part—only physical work mattered. Those people who "worked" in town in banks, offices, and shopping malls had soft jobs. Yet, out in the fields nothing could stop my mind from wandering, imagining a world I had never seen. I wanted to do more, go more, have more, and be more than anything I was seeing.

And as I continued to read Scripture on my own, I began to notice a new perspective on work. If work was a punishment for evil, why does the Bible continuously tell us to enjoy our work? Even Solomon in his most pessimistic moments told us "it is also the gift of God whenever anyone eats, drinks, and enjoys all his efforts" (Eccles. 3:13). In Colossians 3:23 we are told "whatever you do, do it enthusiastically, as something done for the Lord and not for men." And God even seems to be promising work as a reward in eternity. Surprise! The saved will "build houses and live [in them]; they will plant vineyards" and "will fully enjoy the work of their hands" (Isa. 65:21–22).

Although I was expected to continue in the family farming when I completed high school, my own desire for work that seemed a better fit for me led me to college to broaden my options. The disadvantages of a poor, legalistic upbringing were helpful in forcing me to look beyond familial expectations for a more fulfilling life. I began a path of relentless personal study alongside academic requirements for multiple degrees in psychology and religion. I wanted to see if I could blend a life committed to God with a life of meaningful work.

Along the way I have worked as an adjunctive therapist in a psychiatric hospital, taught psychology at the university level, sold cars, owned a 4,000-member health and fitness center, built an auto accessories business, painted houses, mowed lawns, counseled at a church, ran a cashew vending machine business, and sold books and tapes on the Internet.

Today I do life coaching as my core business and have 7 additional complementary businesses. The foundational principles you will read come from personal experience and many years of studying and counseling with those who, like I, have found their calling.

GETTING STARTED

48 Days to the Work You Love outlines a new process of looking at what you are going to be when you grow up. How has God uniquely gifted you in (1) *skills and abilities,* (2) *personality traits,* and (3) *values, dreams, and passions?* From these areas we can see clear patterns from which to make career and job decisions. These patterns create a compass, providing a sense of continuity in the midst of inevitable job changes and workplace unpredictability. Looking inward is 85 percent of the process of finding proper direction; 15 percent is the application to career choices.

Work is not a curse of God but one of the benefits of walking in His will. Finding *the work you love* is not a self-serving goal; it is a required component of fulfilling our true calling.

You may be asking, why *48 Days?* Well, the Bible is quite clear that God considers 40 days to be a spiritually significant time period. In fact, in the Bible, anytime God wanted to prepare people for something better, He took 40 days.

- Noah's life and the world were transformed by 40 days of rain.
- Moses was a different man after spending 40 days on Mount Sinai.
- The Israelite spies scouted the Promised Land for 40 days.
- Elijah ran more than 200 miles in 40 days on 1 meal to get to a place where he could hear from God again.
- Goliath spent 40 days challenging the Israelite army while God prepared David to confront him.
- The people of Nineveh were transformed in 40 days after God's challenge to change their ways.

- Jesus was empowered for ministry by spending 40 days in the desert.
- The disciples were transformed by spending 40 days with Jesus after the Resurrection.
- There are 40 days between Ash Wednesday and Easter (not counting Sundays).

I'm giving you 8 free days in the process to create your own plan. Take a break on Sundays and a couple of Saturdays. Don't knock yourself out; just stay committed to this time frame to avoid the usual procrastination.

The next 48 days can transform your life. Take them to look at how you are uniquely gifted, identify your strongest characteristics, consider the options, choose the best path for meaningful and fulfilling work, create a plan of action, and *act*.

Believing that God created me for His purposes
and scheduled every day of my life,
I commit the next 48 days to a new clarity
and a plan of action for moving into God's calling for me.

_____

Name   *Date*

What Is Work?

The master in the art of living makes little distinction between his work and his play, his labor and his leisure, his mind and his body, his information and his recreation, his love and his religion. He hardly knows which is which. He simply pursues his vision of excellence at whatever he does, leaving others to decide whether he is working or playing. To him he is always doing both.

—JAMES MICHENER

Is work that necessary evil that consumes the time between our brief periods of enjoyment on the weekends? Is it primarily a method of paying the bills and showing responsibility? Or a way to prove to our parents that the college degree was a reasonable investment? Or the shortest path to retirement? Or is it more?

A recent note from a client read:

"Dan, in following the '48 Days to the Work You Love' principles, I realized that only one of my personal goals was being met by my employment; bringing home a salary. I needed an emotional push that would give me permission to break the chains in which I was bound. This process may have saved my life since I was at the point of self-destruction. I felt that I was worth more to my family through collecting insurance than being there for them. Without God's direction and '48 Days' helping me to gain insight into my feelings and explore my dreams, I don't know where I would have ended up."

A highly paid mechanical engineer, this gentleman was responsible and had what would appear to be a successful career path. But the work had become nothing more than a paycheck for him.

The *Encarta* dictionary defines *work* as

1. paid employment at a job,
2. the duties or activities that are part of a job or occupation,
3. the place where somebody is employed, or
4. the time that a person spends carrying out his or her job.

We seem to contrast this definition of work with play. Surely we can escape work to spend time in play.

The same dictionary defines *play* as

1. to engage in enjoyable activity,
2. to deal with a situation in a particular way to achieve a desired result, or
3. to take part in a game or a sporting activity.

To work is to carry out the duties of a job; to play is to do something enjoyable. But what if you found something you truly enjoyed that also supplied your needed income? Would work and play actually become one and the same? Is it unreasonable to expect our work to be an enjoyable activity?

Not Work. Not Play. What Is It?

Recently my good friend Lou was trying to describe a time when he had been off work, not on vacation and not really having fun. "There must be a word," he thought, "to describe that kind of activity."

What would that be? Only 2 describe our daily activities and, unfortunately, we put *work* and *play* at opposite ends of a spectrum. I propose that we create some new words to describe activity in between work and play. What would you call doing a job around the house—*horking?* What about volunteering at your church—*volking?* How would you describe just reading a good book? Or having a meaningful conversation with a friend?

I would like to see a gamut of words from *work* to *play* that more clearly define how we view those activities. Pass your suggestions to me at work@48Days.com. We'll enlighten my friend Lou and perhaps add to the next edition of *Webster's.*

I decided to check a couple other words that are thrown in with work and play. *Leisure* is "time during which somebody has no obligations or work responsibilities, and therefore is free to engage in enjoyable activities." The word comes from a term in an old French dialect—*leissor,* which means "permission," or literally "to be allowed."

Leo Tolstoy, struggling in his search for godliness, looked at the lives of his privileged class and the lives of the plain folks who were their laborers. He determined that whatever their hardships, the working folk rested at night in peace and confidence in God's goodness, while those in royalty frequently complained and were unhappy about their lives. He renounced his wealthy class and set out to work in the fields alongside the peasants. He proclaimed that the greatest error of the leisure class was the erroneous belief that "felicity consists in idleness." In *A Talk Among Leisured People* he asserted that we must return to the recognition "that work, and not idleness, is the indispensable condition of happiness for every human being."

What if you were "allowed" to do what you most enjoyed every day? What would this do to our definition of retirement?

The definition of *retire* is

1. to stop working willingly; to leave a job or career voluntarily;
2. to stop engaging in daily activities and go to bed;
3. to leave a place, position, or way of life and go to a place of less activity; or
4. withdraw something from service.

Isn't that what is implied when people talk about retirement? *When can I stop this stupid job and start doing what I really enjoy?* Do you really want to stop engaging in daily activities? Or withdraw from service? Instead, why not expect enjoyment in your daily work?

The fruits of a fulfilling life—happiness, confidence, enthusiasm, purpose, and money—are mainly by-products of doing something we enjoy, with excellence, rather than things we can seek directly.

In his popular book *The Millionaire Mind,* Thomas J. Stanley, Ph.D., looks at the characteristics of America's wealthiest people, attempting to identify their distinguishing traits. Is it their IQ, GPA, college major, family's opportunity, or business selection? Surprisingly, none of these topics seems to predict their extraordinary success. The one characteristic the millionaires did have in common is *they were all doing something they loved.* Dr. Stanley concludes, "If you love, absolutely love what you are doing, chances are excellent that you will succeed."

Our early ideas of work tend to view it as something less than desirable and enjoyable. Tom, a sharp 27-year-old, came to my office wanting confirmation that he was on the right track. He had recently graduated from college (having finished the 7-year plan) and had taken a sales position with an office-equipment company. Each morning he put on his suit and made his calls. The company loved him, but he was bored beyond belief. I asked him why he had taken this route, and his reply relayed a common perception. Tom said that he had a great time in college—traveling, snowboarding, attending ball games, and spending time with his friends. After graduation, he felt it was time to "grow up" and become part of the "real world." He assumed that meant getting a job he hated to prove his responsibility.

I laughed and asked who had sold him that bill of goods. We looked carefully at his skills, personality traits, values, dreams, and passions. Today, Tom is co-owner of a snowboard shop in Breckenridge, Colorado. On a moonlit night you might catch him coming down a hill, testing one of his new designs.

▶ Abused Wife Syndrome

No, this extract is not really about abused wives, but I had a client use that term recently in describing his repeated return to the unfulfilling work of his professional training. In his mind, there was a strikingly similar pattern. He would break away from the work he despised for something more rewarding, experience a challenge or setback, and return to the dreaded work, knowing it was where he could make the most predictable income.

Do you do your work only because of its paycheck? Do you
long to leave for something more enjoyable? Have you tried
another path only to return to what is more familiar? Many
people often get trapped in these patterns of returning to negative, abusive situations. The emotions and self-esteem issues
there may be complicated and confusing. However, the stakes are
dramatically lessened with a job. A job should not define who or
what you are. You can leave today and not change the overall purpose or direction of your life. Your calling is a much larger concept than what you do daily to create income. Walk away to a
more fulfilling and rewarding job.

WHY DO WE WORK?

In asking this question, I typically get the following responses:
- to pay the bills
- for food, clothing, and shelter
- because of others' expectations
- to combat boredom
- for self-worth
- for social stimulation
- because it's a place to go

I encounter a lot of people who leave their traditional jobs
because they want to do something more significant. One woman,
who has just resigned from her $74,000-per-year job, said she
wanted to do something "noble." Many are saying they want to
make a difference, to make the world a better place, and to do
something with *spiritual* significance.

Now there's another word worth checking out—*spiritual,*
meaning . . .

1. of the soul: relating to the soul or spirit, usually in contrast
   to material things; or
2. temperamentally or intellectually akin: connected by an
   affinity of the mind, spirit, or temperament.

You mean normal work does not connect our mind, spirit, and
temperament? Perhaps we can create a definition of *work* that

includes more than just completing duties for a paycheck. What if we were able to create a model for work that included work, play, leisure, and spiritual components?

Would it be unreasonable to expect to find fulfilling, enjoyable, spiritually significant, income-producing work?

In his book *Prayer,* Richard Foster says, "The work of our hands and of our minds is acted out prayer, a love offering to the living God." St. Augustine adds, "To work is to pray." Is that how you feel about your work—that it's a prayer offering to God? Or are you thinking that perhaps God looks the other way when you go to work?

How is it possible for our work to be a form of prayer? This may seem challenging as long as we think of prayer as something we do only on our knees with folded hands and closed eyes. But if we recognize prayer as a time of being present with God, then it follows that our work can be a form of engaging our hearts and spirits in a way that places us in His presence. Anything less would be a questionable use of our time, talent, and resources.

We live in a time that gives us the luxury of seeing the benefits of work besides just providing a paycheck. The frustration of those even at high-income levels reminds me again and again that money is ultimately never enough compensation for unhappily investing one's time and energy. There must be a sense of purpose, meaning, and accomplishment. Remember psychologist Abraham Maslow's famous hierarchy of needs:

1. First, I need food, water, air, rest, etc. (basic physiological needs).
2. Second, I need *safety* and *security.* (Do I have stability and structure?)
3. I need to *belong* and feel *loved.* (Does anybody like me?)
4. Next comes *self-esteem.* (Do I feel competent and appreciated?)
5. Lastly, I need *self-actualization.* (Am I doing what I'm suited for/talented at?)

Most of us aren't worried about finding food tonight, but we are concerned about how we can do what we're meant to do.

Having a job that provides nothing more than safety and security is not very fulfilling. Work cannot be the only component of a successful, fulfilling life, but it is a very useful tool.

Crushed Spirit

I recently saw a 61-year-old gentleman who lost his job 9 months ago. When a long period of unemployment has passed, I always suspect more life issues to be lurking in the sidelines. Sure enough, his wife left him 4 months ago, his daughter ("the joy of my life") got married and moved away 5 months ago, his investments are now worth less than half of what they were 3 years ago, his place of employment for 36 years let him go with a small severance package, and he's unconnected at his church and feels "rejected on all sides." He made the last mortgage payment 3 weeks ago on his dream house that now must be sold to settle the divorce before he moves into an apartment in town.

Where do we go from there? Proverbs 18:14 tells us "a man's spirit can endure sickness, but who can survive a broken spirit?" Or in the Living Bible "what hope is left?"

Each area of our lives requires us to make deposits of success. Tiny withdrawals with no deposits will lead to physical, spiritual, and emotional bankruptcy in relationships, jobs, and finances. In times of crisis the area of most pain gets most of our attention, but by making extra deposits in other areas, we can bounce back to success in our depleted accounts.

My advice: Set aside time for vigorous physical exercise. Walk 3 miles 4 or 5 times a week—the feeling will help release tension and stimulate creativity. Seek out a godly mentor. Much of the success of Alcoholics Anonymous has been from attendees' having another person to call in the lowest times. Read inspirational material at least 2 hours daily. Volunteer for a worthy cause—helping someone else in need is a great way to ease the inward pain. Get a job even if it's not your dream job or a great career move. Deliver pizzas or work in the garden department at Home Depot to get moving in a positive direction while you continue to build for long-term success.

Unfortunately, some losses are irretrievable and some pain is debilitating. If you recognize too many withdrawals in your life, take drastic measures to stop the hemorrhaging today!

HOW DO WE CHOOSE WORK?

> *"Choose a job you love, and you will never have to work a day in your life."*
> — *Confucius*

The opportunities in today's work environment are endless. While in previous generations children adopted the careers handed down by their parents, today's youth have little or no guidance to direct them onto a work path. They enter the workplace with little work experience and little knowledge of varied careers, leading to poorly made life-directing decisions. Often, a career decision is made with less thought and planning than is put into deciding where to go for spring break. When I asked a young college graduate how he chose criminal justice as his major, he said, "On the first day of college they sent all of us freshmen into a big room. Then they announced, 'If you are going into accounting, follow this lady down the hall. Advertising majors, go this way.' I looked down the list [of majors], closed my eyes, and hit the page with my finger. Criminal justice became my chosen field."

Don't laugh. It's a frequently used process. Who knows how to choose the right major? Many business administration majors discovered during their junior year that the quickest way to graduation was by declaring that major. I'm now starting to see graduates with degrees in university studies. Was it just too challenging to decide on any focus? Next we'll have a degree in showing up. That's why ten years after graduation, 80 percent of college graduates are working in something totally unrelated to their college major. And that's OK. College is a broadening experience that rarely forces anyone into a narrow tunnel of no escape. You can change course several times in a lifetime without feeling like you're derailed or starting over if you have a sense of calling to act as a constant compass. More on that in chapter 3.

▶ "The Shallow Waters of Avarice"

The first request I issue when I coach someone is "Briefly describe your current work situation."

Here is a recent response from a young man: "Antithetical to my personal and professional expectations. Unfulfilling on multiple levels: Lack of meaning and purpose; a myopic pursuit of the almighty dollar; a parasitic and never-ending voyage into the shallow waters of avarice." Wow. What a powerful and eloquent statement of being offtrack and realizing that money is never enough compensation for investing one's time and energy.

He continued: "Because of the necessity and immediacy of my situation . . . I took the path of least resistance, which has led me down a perilous pike of disappointment and despair. As a direct result of our financial obligations, I absolved myself of the freedom to pursue my dreams for the oppressive restraints of debt." Feeling trapped by the realities of life, he felt blocked from any attempts at following his true passions.

Fortunately, new possibilities are possible. We mapped out a process for getting an additional degree and an immediate plan for expression of his unique writing skills. He can hike, run a marathon, study fossils with his kids, and get involved in a book club. Life does not have to be put on hold. There are always ways to make deposits of success in areas deemed important. Few obstacles exist beyond those in our minds if we are creative in looking for solutions. And remember to enjoy the journey, starting with today. Success is not a future event—it is the "progressive realization of worthwhile goals." Thus, either you are successful today or you are not.

Look for opportunities to rise above the "shallow waters of avarice" today.

Generational expectations still do play a large role in many career decisions. Historically each generation has been expected to be more educated and wealthier than the preceding one. Many baby boomers had the finest degrees, invested in the big dot-coms, and banked millions. Now what is their offspring supposed to do to top that? Or here's a situation: What if the son of a cardiologist is really gifted as a carpenter? Can we encourage that young man to be excellent as a carpenter, or will he be railroaded into a "professional" career?

Several years ago I saw a young surgeon who had gone to Harvard Medical School, as had his father and grandfather. He had the finest cars and opportunities along the way. And yet something was amiss. By the time he came to see me, he was shooting heroin into the heels of his feet (the heels being the only parts of his body where he had not abused the veins). He had been admitted to a psychiatric hospital in an attempt to save his life. While working with me, he expressed his childhood dream of driving a truck.

Today he works as an emergency room physician on the weekends and is still able to make a significant income. During the week he drives a snack delivery truck. He has moved out to the country and is getting his life in order.

Proverbs 22:6 says, "Teach a youth about the way he should go; even when he is old he will not depart from it." That verse has been distorted to justify cramming spiritual principles onto impressionable children to make certain their theology matches their parents'. A truer reading of the original text would be: "Train up a child in the way that he/she is bent . . . ." The challenge of parenting is to discover how God has uniquely gifted this child and how the parent can help the child excel in that area. Thus there will be times when the son of a surgeon will be most gifted as a truck driver or carpenter or musician or missionary. Well-intentioned parents, teachers, pastors, and others in positions of influence can easily misdirect an impressionable child if only external opportunities are the criteria for career selection. The power of confidence in career choice comes from looking inward for the alignment of personal characteristics, not from looking outward to where "opportunities" lie.

Here are some more misdirected influences in choosing a career:

- What will be in the most demand? With entire industries becoming obsolete in 4 to 5 years, how can we accurately predict the jobs of the future?
- What is the most secure? *Security* is a slippery concept in today's work environment. Little security is found in any company or job. The only security is in understanding your-self—that will provide a compass for navigating the inevitable changes.
- How can I achieve position, status, and power? This is likely to be an elusive path, leading to rapid burnout.
- Where can I get the greatest income? (Similar to the previous bullet point.) If you look first at the money, it will likely stay just outside your grasp.
- What's advertised in the paper? Probably the worst of all influences, having nothing to do with your uniqueness or a proper alignment of your calling.

None of these will help you build a *life plan*. Be very aware that getting a job is only one tool for creating a meaningful life.

Better questions to ask regarding a career or job choice would be:

- What was I born to do?
- What would be my greatest contribution to others?
- What do I really love to do (and when I'm doing it, time just flies by)?
- What are the recurring themes that I find myself drawn to?
- How do I want to be remembered?

"To thine own self be true, / And it must follow, as the night the day, / Thou canst not then be false to any man." — Shakespeare, Hamlet 1.3.80–82.

When we are not true to ourselves, to our unique God-given characteristics, we lose the power of authenticity, creativity, imagination, and innovation. Our life becomes performance-based, setting the stage for compromise in all other areas of our lives.

COUNTDOWN TO WORK I LOVE

1. Who gave you your first job? What kind of job was it? How much money did you make?
2. From looking at your work life so far, what has been of the greatest value or worth?
3. If your job changes, does your purpose change?
4. Do you think your current job will exist five years from now?
5. What would be the key characteristics of an ideal job or career?
6. When you daydream, what do you see yourself doing?
7. What have been the happiest, most fulfilling moments in your life?
8. If nothing changed in your life in the next 5 years, would that be OK?

The Challenge of Change
React, Respond, or Get Trampled

*A man of character finds a special attractiveness in difficulty,
since it is only by coming to grips with difficulty
that he can realize his potentialities.*

—CHARLES DE GAULLE

*Affliction produces endurance, endurance produces proven character,
and proven character produces hope.*

—ROMANS 5:3–4

"Is there still time for me to make my life count?" Recently I met a 27-year-old who asked me this very question. "Please tell me," he continued, "that just because I started as an attorney doesn't mean my life will be filed away. . . . Encourage me to find a motivating desire once more. I think I've lost it."

Is it too late for this misdirected 27-year-old? When do we reach the point of no return and have to settle for the life we have chosen or had chosen for us?

People are increasingly saying, "I still don't know what I want to do when I grow up." And this is coming not only from the 20-year-olds but from those in their 40s and 50s as well. People often say this with embarrassment, but the search for clear meaning should be a continued one for each of us. If you are still living out your life based on decisions made when you were 18, you should be concerned. Things have changed. You have changed.

WHERE DO JOBS GO?

From 1920 until the mid-80s, getting a job with a large company was the dream of most every young American. The unwritten agreement between the corporation and the employee was, *If you work for us throughout your working lifetime, we will take care of you.*

In the 1980s this unspoken contract disintegrated. Twenty million blue-collar workers, many of whom had spent their entire lives working for one organization, were let go. What happened? Fifty years ago, it took a lifetime for technology to make your job irrelevant—now it takes only 4 to 5 years.

U.S. Department of Labor statistics state that 50 percent of the jobs we will have in the next 6 years have not yet been created. StaffMark, the national temporary-staffing agency, predicts that in the next 4 years, 50 percent of the workforce will be contract labor. *Time* magazine noted that in 2002 approximately 1.2 million jobs were eliminated, or 3,287 every day. And today the average length of a job in America is 3.2 years. That means that in a 45-year working span, a person can be expected to have 14 to 16 different jobs. These changes require that each of us develops a clear sense of who we are and where we are going, or we will feel victimized by those changes. Here's how these facts negatively affect us:

- 70 percent of American workers experience stress-related illnesses.
- 34 percent think they will burn out on the job in the next 2 years, according to the U.S. Department of Health and Human Services.
- There is a 33-percent increase in heart attacks on Monday mornings, according to the *Los Angeles Times.*
- More people die at 9 o'clock Monday morning than any other time of day or any other day of the week, according to the National Centers for Disease Control and Prevention.
- There is a 25-percent increase in work-related injuries on Mondays, according to *Entrepreneur* magazine.
- Male suicides are highest on Sunday nights, with men realizing that their careers—and possibly their finances as well—are not where they want them.

The good news is that small businesses are adding more than 2 million new positions annually, far outweighing the traditional job losses. Yes, these jobs may look different; they may not come with a company car, 401(k), and medical benefits, but they are exciting new opportunities.

NOBODY GETS "FIRED" ANYMORE

In a recent workshop, the terms for being "let go" became the center of attention as participants shared their stories. It seems no one gets fired anymore in this politically correct work environment. Back in 1980 a person got "fired." By 1985 it was "laid off." In 1990 it became "downsized." Now a person can be "rightsized," "restructured," "reorganized," "reengineered," or "put in the mobility pool." I hear that many people are being freed up to "pursue other opportunities." In this computer age, some people are being "uninstalled" and receiving their termination notices via e-mail. One lady shared that she had been on the receiving end of a "cost-containment exercise."

The coldest term I have heard recently is that certain people are informed that they are "surplus." Isn't that a nice feeling after 25 years of faithful service? You are essentially in the same category as a case of Liquid Paper thanks to spell check.

Is it surprising that morale is often low for the remaining employees whose workload has tripled, while their salary remains the same? Are they the "lucky" ones to still be around after all the smart ones took a buy-out package and got better jobs elsewhere?

Everyone lives on the edge of job obsolescence and the threshold of career opportunity. And with every change there is the seed of new opportunity. Yes, not all change is positive growth, but all positive growth does require change. Change is predictable and inevitable, impersonal and relentless. The question is not will change reach you, but *how will you respond?*

Thomas Edison's teachers said he was "too stupid to learn anything." He was fired from his first 2 jobs for being "nonproductive." As an inventor, Edison made 10,000 unsuccessful attempts at inventing the light bulb. When a reporter asked, "How did it feel to fail 10,000 times?" Edison replied, "I didn't fail 10,000 times. The light bulb was an invention with 10,000 steps."

Walt Disney was fired by a newspaper editor because "he lacked imagination and had no good ideas." He went bankrupt several times before he built Disneyland. In fact, the proposed park was rejected by the city of Anaheim on the grounds that it would only attract riffraff.

Our strategy needs to focus on handling the change process and turning it into a positive force.

▶ Do You Want to Be a Butterfly or a Freak?

A man found a cocoon of a butterfly. One day a small opening appeared. He watched the butterfly for several hours as it struggled to force its body through that little hole. Then it seemed to stop making any progress. It appeared as if it could go no further. So the man decided to help the butterfly. He snipped off the remaining bit of the cocoon. The butterfly then emerged easily. But it had a swollen body and small, shriveled wings. The man expected that the wings would enlarge and expand to support the body, which would contract in time, but neither happened. Instead the butterfly spent the rest of its life crawling around with a swollen body and shriveled wings. It never flew. What the man, in his kindness and haste, did not understand was that the restricting cocoon was God's way of forcing fluid from the butterfly's body into its wings, so that it could fly once free from the cocoon.

Sometimes struggles are exactly what we need. If God allowed us to go through our lives without any obstacles, it would cripple us. We would not be as strong and we could never fly!

ANYTIME THERE IS CHANGE, THERE ARE SEEDS OF OPPORTUNITY

Three caterpillars were crawling through a field. Seeing a butterfly pass over them, the first caterpillar said, "Look at that smart aleck up there, flitting around, making us feel stupid." The second caterpillar said, "You know, some days I wish I could fly." The third caterpillar looked up and said excitedly, "I know that guy. He used to be one of us. If he can fly, I know I can too."

Most of us respond to change as one of those caterpillars. Are we threatened? Are we resentful? Or are we excited about the possibilities for our own advancement and success?

Do you see change as a provider of new opportunities or as a threat to expected security? What is "security"? Is it a guaranteed future? A company that provides medical benefits, vacation time, and a retirement plan? Not anymore. Security today is not likely to come from a job, a company, or the government. General Douglas MacArthur said, "Security is your ability to produce."

Contrast MacArthur's definition with George's. George has been with the same company for 23 years but hates his job. He has missed much of his children's lives, works on his wife's day off, and his health is deteriorating. But he can't imagine leaving the "security" of his job.

Now let me tell you how they catch monkeys in Africa. The natives take a coconut and at one end cut a hole just large enough for a monkey's hand to enter. The other end of the coconut is attached to a long rope. They then carve out the inside of the coconut and put a few peanuts inside. They place the coconut in a clearing and hide in the trees with the end of the rope. The monkeys come around, smell the peanuts, and reach inside to grab a fistful. But now, with a fistful, their hand is too large to retract through the small hole. Then the natives yank on the cord and haul that silly monkey to captivity because the monkey will not let go of those few lousy peanuts he thought he wanted.

Your only "security" is knowing what you do well. Knowing your *areas of competence* will give you freedom amid corporate politics and unexpected layoffs.

Wayne Gretzky was once asked why he was such a great hockey player. He responded with an eloquent morsel of wisdom: "I simply went to where the puck *was going to be*." An average player would go where the puck was or is.

Change is inevitable, but there are upsides of change. Forest fires clean out the undergrowth and thus protect the tallest trees from danger. Many environmentalists have been obsessed with preventing any controlled fires to eliminate undergrowth, and consequently, we have seen major forest fires in the last few years. All that undergrowth provides a perfect setting for a major uncontrollable disaster when the inevitable fire does come. Maybe we need the little fires of change in our own lives periodically to keep us less vulnerable to the major changes.

PERSPECTIVE: TRAGEDY OR BLESSING?

Years ago in Scotland, the Clark family had a dream. The husband and his wife worked and saved, making plans for their 9 children and themselves to travel to the United States. After many years, they finally had enough money and passports to make reservations for the family to sail on a new liner to the United States.

The family was filled with anticipation and excitement about their new life. But 7 days before their departure, the youngest son was bitten by a dog. The doctor sewed up the boy but hung a yellow sheet on the Clark's front door, signaling a household quarantine for 14 days because of the possibility of rabies.

The family's dreams were dashed. They couldn't make the trip to America as planned. The father, filled with disappointment and anger, stomped to the dock to watch the ship leave without the Clark family. He shed tears of disappointment and cursed both his son and God for their misfortune.

Five days later, the tragic news spread throughout Scotland—the mighty *Titanic* had sunk. The unsinkable ship had taken hundreds of lives. The Clark family was to have been on that ship, but because the son had been bitten by a dog, they were left behind in Scotland.

When the father heard the news, he ran home, hugged his son, and thanked him for saving the family. He thanked God for saving their lives and turning what he knew was a tragedy into a blessing.

How many times have you been disappointed or angry at what seemed to be a defeat or failure? Have you ever later discovered that the failure saved you from a bigger disaster or directed you to something even better? Do you view failure as starting over, or do you look for the better direction and a better opportunity based on what you now know?

Many times in coaching people toward better careers, I find that a job loss or business failure, while devastating at first, is later viewed as the best thing that ever happened. Guard against letting setbacks embitter you. Look for the seeds of opportunity in that situation. Build on what you know and approach that new mountain to scale.

GET OFF THE NAIL!

A neighbor saw an old dog lying on a front porch. Hearing the dog softly moaning, the neighbor approached the porch. He asked the owner why the dog was whimpering. The owner said, "He's lying on a nail." The neighbor asked, "Well, why doesn't he move?" To which the owner replied, "I guess it doesn't hurt quite that much yet."

A lot of people are like that old dog. They moan and groan about their situation but don't do anything. How bad does the pain have to get before you get up and do something else? If you are in a negative environment, take a fresh look at yourself, define where you want to be, and develop a clear plan of action for getting there.

Change, even if unwelcome, forces us to reevaluate what our best options are. Those times of transitions are great opportunities to look for recurring patterns in your life and make adjustments to build on the good and reduce the bad.

We easily become creatures of habit. A train creates a tremendous amount of momentum to keep moving along the same track. It takes an unusual or unexpected force to redirect that train. That's why without change in some form we are likely to simply continue on the same path.

Often in working with professionals, I am reminded of how difficult it is for them to see things in new ways. They become so accustomed to doing the same things in the same ways that any change is perceived as life-threatening, even if the current situation is frustrating or negative. They have so much training in narrow thinking that anything different is intimidating.

Dealing with Obstacles in Our Path

In ancient times, a king, wanting to test his subjects, placed a boulder in the main road leading to his city. Then he hid himself and watched to see people's reactions. Some of the king's wealthiest merchants and courtiers came by and simply walked around it. Many loudly blamed the king for not keeping the roads clear. None did anything about getting the big stone out of the way. Then a peasant came along, carrying a load of vegetables. On approaching the boulder, the peasant laid down his burden and tried to move the stone to the side of the road. After much pushing and straining, he finally succeeded. As the peasant picked up his load of vegetables, he noticed a purse lying in the road where the boulder had been. The purse contained gold coins and a note from the king, indicating that the gold was for the person who removed the boulder from the road. The peasant learned what many others never understand: taking initiative presents unexpected rewards.

"Obstacles are those frightful things you see when you take your eye off the goal."
— *Hannah More,*
quoted in
Multiple Streams of Income
by Robert G. Allen

If you ask a group of 30 second-graders, "How many of you can draw, sing, or dance?" every hand will go up as everyone clamors for a chance to prove their multiple abilities. Ask the same group when they are juniors in high school and perhaps half will claim any one of these skills. Ask the same group when they're at age 35, and you will find perhaps 2 or 3 who acknowledge performing adequately in any of these areas. What happened? Did they all lose their earlier abilities? No, we get used to very familiar paths in our lives and eliminate many possibilities along the way.

Much of my success as a life coach is in helping people once again see new possibilities; to consider solutions they have never before considered. Unexpected change can help initiate this process.

COMMON CAREER QUESTIONS

1. *Should I find a job and stay with it until I retire?*

   As mentioned earlier, the average job in America is now 3.2 years long, and the average American worker will have 14 to 16 different jobs in his or her working lifetime. You must develop a sense of what you can contribute that goes beyond only 1 company or organization. A career path today will likely involve moving from organization to organization, creating a picture of rising circles, rather than a vertical ladder. In fact, a vertical rise within one organization will very likely move you away from your strongest areas of competence.

2. *Do I have to deal with change?*

   Change is inevitable. It is relentless and nondiscriminating. Our only choice is how we are going to respond to it. If you know your strongest competencies, are prepared, and have a clear focus, you will have a sense of continuity—not a feeling of starting over each time you are confronted with a job change.

3. *How can I keep my job from controlling my life?*

   First decide what kind of life you want, then plan your work around that life. Make sure you build in balanced priorities. Exchange your time for valued priorities not only money. Move away from the idea that more time equals more success. If you are working more than 45 to 50 hours a week in your job, you are limiting success in some other areas of your life. Don't expect all your fulfillment, value, and meaning to come from the work you do.

Make sure you are making deposits of success in all 7 areas of your life (see chap. 4).

4. *What if I don't want another corporate job? Do I have other options?*

   Many people are switching to new work models. Estimates show that currently 60 percent of American homes are housing some kind of business, according to the National Federation of Independent Business (NFIB). In the next 5 years, that number will grow dramatically. There are many choices for businesses you can run yourself (see chap. 10). In addition, there are many varieties of work models available: consultants, freelance workers, temps, independent contractors, etc.

5. *I don't have a college education. What can I do?*

   Recognize that people get promotions and opportunities in companies due to personal skills—attitude, enthusiasm, self-discipline, and interpersonal expertise—85 percent of the time. Technical or educational skills and credentials get you ahead only 15 percent of the time. Today's work environment creates a level playing field. If you have the personal skills, you can do most anything you want.

6. *Should I stop sending résumés to authors of classified ads?*

   Only about 12 percent of the positions available ever appear in the paper. Learn how to find jobs before they make the paper. The major difference between a successful and unsuccessful job-hunter is not education, age, skill, or ability, but the way he goes about his job search (see chap. 7).

7. *My résumé has me in a rut I can't get out of. What can I do?*

   Rebuild your résumé, highlighting your transferable areas of competence instead of just listing your job descriptions. Show your proficiencies in administration, planning, sales, marketing, training, supervising, financial analysis, etc. These skills are transferable from 1 industry or profession to another (see chap. 6).

EXAMPLES OF CHANGE

This case scenario of a catsup company in St. Louis shows how business is not declining, but it sure is changing.

Catsup company changes over a 10-year period:

- Year 1: $100 million per year in sales with 960 employees.
- Year 2: Cheaper to have an outside printer do barcode labels. Let 20 printing employees go.
- Year 3: Started using specialized bottlecap maker; new seal extends shelf life from 14 to 24 months. Would not sell the equipment—only finished bottle caps. Let 45 bottle cap makers go.
- Year 4: New plastic bottle supplier appeared. Offered for 30 percent less per bottle to mix the catsup, fill the plastic bottle, put on labels, and package bottles for shipping.
- Year 10: $300 million per year in sales with 25 employees. Cost to the company per bottle of catsup now one-third of what it had been 10 years before. Company reduced price by 50 percent. Sales had risen to $300 million with only 25 high-level managers to coordinate agreements with suppliers.

In this real-life example, the company dramatically increased its revenues, while laying off 97 percent of its workforce. However, those 935 workers are not just sitting on the sidewalk; they have been absorbed into new, different companies.

The good news is, the number of small businesses likely to absorb these displaced workers has grown dramatically in the last 15 years to approximately 24.5 million. In the last 10 years, small business has accounted for 71 percent of the nation's new job growth, adding more than 2 million new jobs each year, or 5,479 each day. Small businesses now employ 54 percent of the American workforce. What we are seeing is a healthy return to the kind of business on which our country was founded.

In the Nashville, Tennessee, Metropolitan Statistical Area (a typical American city), 52.8 percent of all the companies repre-sented have 1 to 4 employees. Only 2.6 percent of the companies have 99 or more employees. These numbers show a major change from the emphasis on big corporations in which a company car, 401(k) plan, health care benefits, and long-term "security" were expected components. If your job search targets only those corporations, you are probably targeting only 2.6 percent of the companies out there. Broaden and strengthen your job search by including small, streamlined companies in your target list.

So What Are You Doing While You're Unemployed?

In 1934, Charles B. Darrow of Germantown, Pennsylvania, was unemployed. To amuse himself and pass the time, he created a board game that provided the possibility of fame and fortune. That game is called "Monopoly." Today, it's the best-selling board game in the world, sold in 80 countries and produced in 26 languages.

Incidentally, he originally presented it to the executives at Parker Brothers, but they rejected the game due to "52 design flaws"! But Mr. Darrow wasn't daunted; his situation and personal passion for the game inspired him to produce it on his own.

With help from a friend who was a printer, Darrow sold 5,000 handmade sets of the game to a Philadelphia department store. People loved it! But as demand grew, he couldn't keep up with all the orders and revisited Parker Brothers. The rest, as they say, is history. In its first year, 1935, the "Monopoly" game was the best-selling game in America. And over its 65-year history, an estimated 500 million people have played it.

So what are you doing while you're unemployed? One good idea is all you need to change your life!

DEALING WITH CHANGE

You may be asking yourself some tough questions:
- Is this really all there is?
- Am I doing what God wants me to do?
- Does my life have a purpose?
- Did I make a wrong turn somewhere?

Are you ready for change?

The best way to deal with the challenge of change is to be prepared to respond.

First, look at yourself. The more you understand yourself, the more you can move forward with boldness and confidence.

When you get to heaven, God is not going to ask you why you weren't more like Mother Teresa. He's likely to ask you why you weren't more like you. Your responsibility and source of real freedom and success is to discover who you are. Lead with your own unique talents and personality. Be authentically you and let God use you.

> *"The unexamined life is not worth living."*
> — *Socrates*

Last night I returned from a meeting to find my wife and daughter watching the movie, *Forrest Gump*. At one part, Jenny asks, "What are you gonna be when you grow up?" and Forrest says, "Why can't I be me?"

I recently received a note from a person who asked how to stop wanting things that he couldn't get in life.

That is either a very painful or a very misguided question. How do you stop wanting those things that you want? How do you become numb to the desires of your heart? Should you just find a job that pays the bills and try to forget doing something you really enjoy? I think not! Clarify what you want, create a plan of action, and begin to walk toward the goal you want.

The power of knowing yourself acts as a compass through change. Popular writer Stephen Covey says the only way we can handle change around us is to know what is *changeless* about ourselves. You need that changeless core, knowing how God has uniquely gifted you and what you value. With that knowledge you can forge through change with clear direction and unshakeable purpose.

> *"The secret of success is focus of purpose."*
> — *Thomas Edison*

Finding a job is a meaningless process until you develop a clear focus that is suited to you.

Just because you have the *ability* to do something does not mean that it is well-suited to you. This is a very significant point that cannot be stressed enough. Many people have been misdirected because they had the ability to do something well. At this stage in your life, you probably have the ability to successfully do 100 to 200 different things career-wise.

Dennis is a 43-year-old dentist. Last year he made more than $300,000. His practice is growing, and his "success" is reflected in his beautiful house and the vacations he and his family take. However, he is also being treated for depression and is increasingly overtaken by panic attacks and the dread of going to the office. In working through this process, we discovered that while Dennis has the ability to be a dentist, he is living out his parents' dream, not his own. He has now sold his dental practice and has gone back to school to get his degree in family counseling.

Genius is the ability to clearly visualize the objective.

The Grace of Interruption

This phrase was reported recently by a lady who had been laid off unexpectedly. She related that she had been given "the grace of interruption." If we look at those words, it really does imply a very positive occurrence. *Grace* is defined as "an attractive quality," "the condition of being favored," or even "a short prayer in which blessing is asked." Surely any of these are to be desired. An *interruption* is "a break in continuity" or "an intermission." Think of a football game intermission in which players review what has happened and then plan for better results in the second half. The refreshing pause helps you become newly focused and energized.

Rather than the panic of feeling fired, perhaps you or someone you know has been given the gift of the grace of interruption.

CHANGE IS COMING—READY OR NOT

- The work world is rife with volatility. People will increasingly work at one career, retire for awhile when they can

afford it, begin another career, and so on in endless varia-
tions. True retirement will be delayed until very late in life.

- Health care benefits are being eliminated. More and more
  people will continue working simply to cover the cost of
  ongoing health care.

- The Bureau of Labor Statistics predicts there will be 50
  million new jobs in the next 4 years, but they can't tell us
  what 50 percent of those jobs will be.

- In the next 6 years we will need 6,000 new schools and
  190,000 additional teachers in the United States. And yet
  teachers are leaving the confrontational classrooms in
  droves.

- In 10 years, 90 percent of what an engineer is taught in college will be available on the computer. In electronics, 50
  percent of what a student learns as a freshman is obsolete
  by his senior year.

- There has been a dramatic change from "production
  workers" to "knowledge workers." Most of us already get
  paid for what we think and create rather than for how
  many railroad ties we can place in a day.

- We're also seeing a dramatic swing from being paid for
  time to being paid for *results*. Keep in mind how recently
  being paid by the hour actually came into place; it was
  only with the introduction of the assembly line that
  people expected to be paid for their time. We are seeing
  a return to the kind of businesses our country was
  founded on.

- Seniority no longer counts—only productivity.

- Nearly 5 million American workers are using the Internet
  as a primary component of their daily job.

- 20 million Americans are telecommuting, working from a
  location distant from the company headquarters.

- Electronic immigrants are now competing for jobs around
  the world. With computers, faxes, and cell phones, work
  can be completed with no geographic barriers. So customer
  service, data input, and even medical radiology and lab

work are being done in distant countries, often with greatly reduced labor costs.

As a result of this volatility in the workplace, many people are misplaced and underemployed. The popular cliché, "Thank God it's Friday," seems to sum up the American feeling about work. Work is a bitter pill, an inevitable evil, and necessary only as a tradeoff to do what we really enjoy. Unfortunately, it even seems a badge of honor to hate your job and despise the boss.

There has to be a better outlook to how we spend the largest block of our time each week.

"ALL BEGINNINGS ARE HOPEFUL!"

This is actually a quote from the president of Oxford University, spoken to entering freshman in 1944 in the midst of a world war. In coaching people going through change, I am often struck by their discouragement, frustration, and resentment. I have come to recognize, however, that those feelings reveal that the person is looking backward—at something that has already occurred. As soon as we are able to create a clear plan for the future, those feelings dissipate and are replaced by hope, optimism, and enthusiasm. In all my years of coaching, I have never seen a person who has a clear plan and goals who is also depressed. They just don't go together.

Viktor Frankl, in his wonderful little book *Man's Search for Meaning,* relates his observations of people in German concentration camps. Age, health, education, or ability could not predict who would survive the atrocities there. Rather it was attitude—only those who believed that there was something better coming tomorrow were able to survive and ultimately walk away from those camps.

Feeling discouraged? Miserable in your job? Just lost your business? Give yourself a new beginning tomorrow. All beginnings are hopeful.

COUNTDOWN TO WORK I LOVE

1. Respond to the statement, "All progress requires change, but not all change is progress."
2. What statement describes your career path so far?
3. How has a company change affected you? How did it make you feel?
4. Have you experienced any "failure" in your career? If so, what did it lead to?
5. What were your childhood goals and ambitions for life? Which ones have you been able to fulfill?
6. Who are 2 or 3 people you know who seem to have accomplished their dreams? What do you remember about their accomplishments?
7. What do you imagine your retirement will be like?

Creating a Life Plan

Work is love made visible.
And if you cannot work with love but only with distaste,
it is better that you should leave your work and sit at the gate of the temple
and take alms of those who work with joy.
For if you bake bread with indifference, you bake a bitter bread
that feeds but half man's hunger.
And if you grudge the crushing of the grapes,
your grudge distills a poison in the wine.
And if you sing though as angels, and love not the singing,
you muffle man's ears to the voices of the day and the voices of the night.
All work is empty save when there is love;
and when you work with love you bind yourself to yourself,
and to one another, and to God.

—KAHLIL GIBRAN, *THE PROPHET*

As a pastor of a growing church, Rob was fulfilling the multiple duties of a pastor; he was the teacher, encourager, comforter, hospital visitor, administrator, and friend. Surely there could be no better expression of a godly calling. Coming from a blue-collar family, Rob had the desire to make a difference, to lead people to godly lives, to be recognized in the community, and to provide financially for his wife and children. And yet Rob was experiencing tremendous unrest. He was quick-tempered at home and frustrated with the demands of his congregation. Financial strains were constant. Rob was determined to hang on to what surely was his calling. Didn't open doors themselves confirm the accuracy of his direction?

Or do they? How do we develop a clear sense of direction regarding our careers? Are open doors, family influence, educational opportunity, and new technologies the best determinants of our direction?

IS YOUR JOB YOUR CALLING?

Here's a framework for moving toward decisions for our work. Three words are used interchangeably and shouldn't be: *vocation, career,* and *job.*

VOCATION

Vocation is the most profound of the three, incorporating calling, purpose, mission, and destiny. This is the big picture many people never identify for themselves. It's what you're doing in life that makes a difference and builds meaning for you, which you can review in your later years to see the impact you've made on the world. Stephen Covey says that we all want "to live, to love, to learn, and to leave a legacy." Our vocation will leave a legacy. The word *vocation* comes from the Latin *vocare,* which means "to call." It suggests that you are listening for something that is calling out to you—something that is particular to you. A calling is something you have to listen for, attuning yourself to the message. Vocation then is not so much pursuing a goal as it is listening for a voice. Before I can tell my life what I want to do with it, I must listen for that voice telling me who I am. Vocation does not come from willfulness but from listening.

> *"Based on the gift they have received, everyone should use it to serve others, as good managers of the varied grace of God."*
> — 1 Peter 4:10

Everyone has a vocation or calling. It's not something reserved for a chosen few who end up as pastors, priests, or monks. As Thomas Merton put it, "A tree gives glory to God by being a tree. For in being what God means it to be it is obeying Him." In the same way, we fulfill our calling by being excellent at whatever God created us to be. Everything you do ought to be part of fulfilling your vocation. Your job will ideally be one part of that, but at times may not be directly related to it.

Anyone can do a "job." You can follow the instructions for drawing a stick person, but the result will not likely be classified as great art. As God was giving Moses detailed plans for building the tabernacle in Exodus, He said, "I have placed wisdom within every skilled craftsman in order to make all that I have commanded you": . . . Moses then said . . . "Look, the LORD has appointed by name Bezalel. . . . He has filled him with God's Spirit, with wisdom, understanding, and ability in every kind of craft to design artistic works in gold, silver, and bronze, to cut gemstones for mounting, and to carve wood for work in every kind of artistic craft" (Exod. 31:6; 35:30–33). Now that's the kind of foundation I want to bring to my work. Not just human ability but godly wisdom and understanding! Machines can do many of our jobs, but vocations flow from the heart of a person who has tapped into that godly wisdom.

CAREER

> "Where the spirit does not work with the hand there is no art."
> — Leonardo da Vinci

If you look at the derivations of the words *vocation* and *career* you will immediately get a feel for the difference between them. *Career* comes originally from the Latin word for "cart" and later from the Middle French word for "racetrack." *Webster's* dictionary defines *career* as "to run or move at full speed, rush wildly." In other words, you can go really fast for a long time but never get anywhere. That is why in today's work environment, even physicians, attorneys, CPAs, dentists, and engineers may choose to get off the expected track and choose another career. A career is a line of work but not the only way to fulfill your calling. You can have different careers at different points in your life. Conversely, two or three different careers can all support your calling.

For example, to embrace the calling of "helping to reduce pain and suffering in the world," we could list multiple careers: physician, nurse, counselor, pastor, teacher, scientist, politician, writer, etc. Thus, if you want to change careers at some point in life, simply take a fresh look at your vocation and find a new application.

JOB

A job is the most specific and immediate of the three terms. It has to do with one's daily activities that produce income. The dictionary defines *job* as "a lump portion, a task, chore or duty." As previously mentioned, the average job is 3.2 years in length, meaning the average person will have 14 to 16 different jobs in his/her working lifetime. So, although the job cannot be the critical definition of your vocation or calling, it should be an expression of that calling and an integration of your ministry.

There is a Hebrew word, *avodah,* from which come the words "work" and "worship." To the Hebrew man, his Thursday morning activities were just as much an expression of worship as being in the synagogue on the Sabbath. Nothing in Scripture depicts the Christian life as divided into sacred and secular parts. Rather, it shows a unified life, one of wholeness, in which everything we do is service to God, including our daily work, whatever that may be.

Jobs will come and go, but they should never derail you from the fulfillment of your calling.

Good career decisions have to be based on more than a casual look at the job opportunities or at personal aptitudes. What we invest our time in daily and weekly must incorporate the three critical areas mentioned in the introduction: (1) *skills and abilities,* (2) *personality tendencies,* and (3) *values, dreams and passions.* The most common mistake people make in choosing a career is doing something simply because they are good at it. The accountant who is good at math or the sales person who is a persuader may still be frustrated because that career forces them to be gregarious or to promote a product they are not excited about. Remembering the happiest times in your life and the times when you felt most fulfilled are better indicators of your calling than just knowing what you can do. Circumstances alone are not good predictors of God's calling. Many people responded to circumstances early in life, and then at 45 are realizing the true components of their calling are missing in their work.

In the case of Rob, a frustrated pastor, we were able to identify his passion for painting beautiful works of art. However, the challenge of providing for a wife and 5 children seemed to make painting and drawing impractical, another issue that frequently misdirects people from their calling. Today, no longer a pastor, he does faux finishes on the walls of elegant homes, creating beautiful effects using sponges, rags, and brushes. He creates dramatic works of art with a musical theme that explode with his spiritual passion. He is making 8 to 10 times the income he was generating previously and is able to "minister" in a way more authentic and fitting for him. As a pastor, he relates that people knew what to expect of him. Now he is the artist, having unique opportunities to relate to many people. They openly share their hurts, frustrations, and vulnerabilities in ways they never did to the "pastor." He now understands that a church-related job is not more "godly" if it is not right for him. God gifts each of us with unique characteristics. Understanding our skills and abilities, our personality tendencies, and our values, dreams, and passions is the first step in identifying the right job.

As Martin Luther recommended: "I advise everyone against entering any religious order or the priesthood unless he is forearmed with this knowledge and understands that the works of monks and priests, however holy and arduous they may be, do not differ one whit in the sight of God from the works of the rustic laborer in the field or the woman going about her household tasks, but that all works are measured before God by faith alone."

Imagine three line workers at the Nissan plant here in middle Tennessee. Each is asked, "What are you doing?" The first responds, "I'm a welder—that's what they pay me for each Friday" (Job). The second says, "I'm making a beautiful car today" (Career). The third worker is thoughtful for a moment and then responds, "I'm helping to create innova-

"Your eyes saw me when I was formless; all [my] days were written in Your book and planned before a single one of them began."
— Psalm 139:16

tive and responsible transportation for individuals, families, and companies" (Vocation). These three workers, all doing the same work, define *job, career,* and *vocation* because of their differing perspectives. If you approach the understanding of your vocation first, you will find tremendous freedom in recognizing how many jobs can fulfill that vocation.

THE BIBLE'S PERSPECTIVE ON WORK

The Bible gives dignity to any work. All occupations are sacred. "Called to ministry" or "full-time service" are simply cultural misrepresentations of God's view of meaningful work. We need to eliminate the artificial ranking of the godliness of work. There are no second-class citizens in the workplace. I thank God for the talents of our lawn maintenance man and greatly appreciate and admire the beauty he creates in the grass, flowers, and trees around our home.

And I am worn out by getting one more letter from someone who suddenly discovered he was "called into full-time service." That immediately creates the false dichotomy of those who are called and those who are not. I might also add that it's interesting how many people discover their call to ministry (meaning they need those who are still *just working* to support them) after a long period of unemployment. Is God's call a last resort? Should it not be a first choice?

PUTTING "WORK" IN PERSPECTIVE

Most Americans evaluate their lives in retrospect, having no clear sense of control, purpose, or destiny for the future. Without knowing where you are going, you are doomed to do likewise.

Here are some revealing statements about where people see themselves:

- 51-year-old businessman—"I feel like I've lived my whole life by accident."
- Wife of professor—"I feel like we've been free-falling for the last 13 years."
- Salesman—"I feel like I'm a ball in a pinball machine."

- 56-year-old bus driver with a Ph.D. in theology—"I feel like I've been given 6 seconds to sing, and I'm singing the wrong song."
- 53-year-old businessman—"I feel like my life is a movie that's almost over, and I haven't even bought the popcorn yet."
- Collection agent—"I've lived my life up until now as though driving with the parking brake on."
- 46-year-old "successful" car salesman—"I feel like a lost ball in tall cotton."
- 39-year-old automotive engineer—"I'm a butterfly caught in a spider's web, with my life slowly being sucked out."
- 27-year-old computer specialist—"I'm a box of parts and nothing fits together."
- 31-year-old attorney—"Law school sucked all the life and creativity out of me."
- 32-year-old in the family business—"The merry-go-round of my professional life has left me no farther than a few steps from where I got on and with a weak stomach."

These are frequent feelings among even "successful" people. It is quite common to reach that point in life where you need to take a fresh look at what you are doing and where you are going.

▶ Learning to Get Back Up

When a baby giraffe is born, within a few seconds it struggles to its feet. Shortly afterward, however, the mother will knock it over from its wobbly stance. This process is repeated each time the baby struggles to its feet until the young giraffe has the strength to stand on its own without falling. What seems like an unkind act is of vital importance to the survival of the young animal. It is, in fact, an act of love by the mother for its child. For the baby giraffe, the world is a dangerous place and it must learn without delay how to quickly get back on its feet.

The late Irving Stone, who spent a lifetime studying the lives of great men such as Michelangelo, Vincent van Gogh, and others, noted a common characteristic of all great men: "You cannot destroy these people," he said. "Every time they're knocked down, they stand up."

A clear sense of purpose will provide a feeling of continuity and contentment to carry you through those inevitable changes. Developing a clear focus leads to confidence, boldness, and enthusiasm in living. If you cannot visualize what you want the future to be, you are likely to end up feeling like a victim of circumstances. If you want different results, you must change what you are doing. In fact, *insanity* is defined as continuing to do the same things and expecting different results.

"Life is never made unbearable by circumstances, but only by lack of meaning and purpose."
— *Viktor Frankl*

If you know where you are going, you can respond to *priorities* rather than *circumstances*. Develop a long-term perspective; don't be like the farmer in Aesop's fable of the goose and the golden egg. The farmer, having become impatient with getting only 1 golden egg a day, decided to cut the goose open and get all the eggs at once. Obviously, not understanding that headless geese don't lay eggs, he cut off the opportunity to get anymore golden eggs. We are in a society that emphasizes instant everything: microwaves, fax machines, cell phones, and coffee. Real personal success comes not in that instant fashion but by careful planning for the long-term future.

Also, when we talk about success, we are talking about balance and success in more areas of life than just career and finances. Too many people have sacrificed success in one area for success in another. Stay committed to achieving success in multiple areas of your life.

A MAN WITH A TOOTHACHE

Shakespeare once stated, "A man with a toothache cannot be in love," meaning simply that the attention demanded by the toothache doesn't allow him to notice anything other than his pain. In working with people going through job change, I often find Shakespeare's principle to be confirmed. I see grown men ignoring their wives, avoiding their friends, watching too much TV, and overeating. I see women stop going to church, spend money they do not have, read romance novels rather than inspirational material, and snap at their kids when asked an innocent question. The "pain" of the job needs seem to overwhelm the health, vitality, and success they have in other life areas.

Going through job change provides a great opportunity to take a fresh look at your success in other areas. Make additional deposits of success in your physical well-being. The energy and creativity that can come from a sharp mind and body can generate the very ideas you need at this time. Take the kids for a cheap meal and enjoy the time together. Organize a pot luck with a group of your friends—you'll be surprised how many of them are going through a similar experience. Pick up a great book to read. Even if you read only 10 minutes a day, you can read a new book a month—and that can transform your insight and preparation for new options. Stay connected spiritually. You'll realize that in the scope of eternity, this event is probably a tiny spot on the time line.

Our common American model has been:

In this model, the job is central. We are frequently more defined by *what we do* than by *who we are*. When meeting a new person, the conversation normally goes as follows: "Hi, John, I'm Dan. What do you do?" From that one brief answer, we make conclusions about that person's intelligence, education, income, and value to society. With this model, we get our total sense of worth from our work. All other aspects of our lives are forced to fit in around the job . . . if there is time. This leads to feelings of resentment, frustration, loss of control, and lack of balance. It also leaves us very vulnerable in that if something happens to that job, whether by circumstances or by our own choice, then we wonder, "Who am I?" That is what happens when our total identity and sense of worth are in our jobs.

What we need is a paradigm shift to:

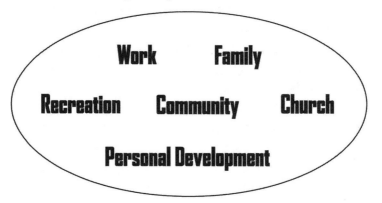

Work　　　Family

Recreation　Community　　Church

Personal Development

Yes, your *job-work-vocation-career* has to incorporate how God has gifted you, what you want to accomplish, and how you want to be remembered. However, you need success equally in those other areas as well. You need a *life plan* with balance not only a *job*. Remember, a job is simply one tool for a successful life.

Your goal should be to plan your *work* around your life, rather than planning your *life* around your work.

The Rat Race—Improve Your Life; Think Like a Rat

We talk about being in the rat race, but this statement is actually demeaning to the rats. Rats won't stay in a race when it's obvious that there's no cheese. The best-seller *Who Moved My Cheese* showed how even smart rats quickly look for new routes to follow when the cheese is gone. Humans, on the other hand, seem to get themselves into traps from which they never escape.

Some research shows that up to 70 percent of white-collar workers are unhappy with their jobs—ironically, they are also spending more and more time working.

Jan Halper, a Palo Alto psychologist, has spent 10 years
exploring the careers and emotions of more than 4,000 male
executives. He found that 58 percent of those in middle management felt they had wasted many years of their lives struggling to
achieve their goals. They were bitter about the many sacrifices
they had made during those years.

Rats, however, move on once they realize the cheese is gone
or perhaps was never there. Rats would probably be embarrassed to be labeled as "being in the human race" for doing
ridiculous things like continuing to go to a job that they hated
every day.

Looking at areas other than your career helps you develop
clear patterns and commonalties that then help define what your
career/job/business/vocation ought to be. This really is a reverse
process but one that leads to true fulfillment. Too often, people
choose a career or line of work because Uncle Bob did it or
because they heard that you could make a lot of money doing it.

I Just Work for the Money

"I've never been happy practicing law." "I have never had a
sense of purpose." "I feel destined to do something great but
have no idea why or what." "I work only for the money."

These are statements from a young attorney, who in his last
position had been sick for 6 months due to an illness "triggered
initially by stress." But a new "career opportunity" presented
itself, and he is now working in a prestigious position with a
Fortune 500 company. Unfortunately, the sickness is returning,
starting with the symptoms of a choking feeling and shortness of
breath.

Ultimately, money is never enough compensation for investing
our time and energy. We need a sense of meaning, purpose, and

accomplishment. Anything that does not blend our values, dreams, and passions will cause us, on some level, to choke. A life well lived must go beyond just making a paycheck—even if it's a very large one.

The Bible tells us in Ecclesiastes 5:10 that "the one who loves money is never satisfied with money, and whoever loves wealth [is] never [satisfied] with income. This too is futile." If money is the only reward of your job, you will begin to see deterioration in your life physically, emotionally, spiritually, and relationally.

I have to add an interesting side note. Proper alignment in doing work we love does not mean our families will be eating rice and beans. In fact, proper alignment releases not only a sense of peace and accomplishment, but money is likely to break in on you like an exploding dam.

In summary:

- Recognize that your career is not your life. It is simply one tool for a successful life.
- Don't put all your energies into one area. Be committed to achieving success in all areas of life.
- Our physical health has a direct relationship to the energy and creativity we bring to our work.

Put your dream and a detailed plan of action into creating a new future.

A plan of action will separate you from 97 percent of the people you meet. Everyone has dreams, but very few ever turn those into goals. The difference between a dream and a goal is that a goal is a dream with a timeframe of action attached.

COUNTDOWN TO WORK I LOVE

1. In today's rapidly changing work environment, is it realistic to expect a job to provide more than just a paycheck?
2. Have you ever had a sense of calling in your life? How did you *hear* that calling?
3. Does God call only a few people?

4. Is it reasonable to expect our work to be part of the fulfillment of our calling?
5. Do you currently have a job, a career, or a vocation?
6. What does *success* mean for you this year?
7. Are you where you thought you'd be at this stage of life?
8. Do you go home at night with a sense of meaning, purpose, and accomplishment?
9. If you want different results next year, what will you change in what you are doing now?

4

PAGE

57

Wheels, Goals, and Clear Action

Work should, in fact, be thought of as a creative activity undertaken for the love of the work itself; and that man, made in God's image, should make things, as God made them, for the sake of doing well a thing that is well worth doing. . . . Work is the natural exercise and function of man—the creature who is made in the image of his Creator.

—DOROTHY L. SAYERS, *WHY WORK?*

"SANCTIFIED IGNORANCE"

Pastor Jones sat in my office, slouched down in the big chair, struggling to relay the events of the last few days. After 19 years of faithful service as a pastor, he had been informed that his contract would not be renewed. No matter how gentle the delivery, the message screamed out at him—he had been fired. How could this happen to a man of God? A man who had committed his life to serving God in the most socially recognized path of service. The anger and sense of betrayal came exploding out as we began to explore his options for moving on.

The portrayal of the preceding years, however, relayed a series of red flags that had been ignored. Pastor Jones was now grossly overweight, having drowned some of his frustrations in eating. He was on medication for depression and was being treated for a bleeding ulcer. Were these not clear signs of a life out of balance? Doesn't God use physical unrest as a method of telling us something is out of alignment? In questioning this gentle, godly man about his current life picture, I discovered his naive theological view. He simply thought that if he were committed to God, somehow everything would just work out. He said he was guilty of "sanctified ignorance." This phrase jumped out at me and has haunted me ever since.

Sanctified ignorance is the belief that if we love God and have committed our lives to Him, everything will work out. And sanctified ignorance is immature theology. If you get up each morning with a clean slate, being open to whatever may happen that day, you will live a life of mediocrity. It is not the path of accomplishment, of excellence, of maximizing our impact and witness. The path of least resistance—just going where it seems easiest to go—creates very crooked streams and very frustrated Christians. The truly godly life is one of focused purpose, having, like Paul, defined the goal and created a plan for its accomplishment.

Knowing God's will is not some passive guessing game. Rather it is taking what God has already revealed to us and developing a plan of action. And God's revelation to us comes through our bodies, minds, hearts, and spirits. Yes, we are submissive to God's will, but God is not an angry taskmaster. He will not force you to be miserable day after day. The secret to creating a career that is both nurturing to the soul and the pocketbook is, as theologian Frederick Buechner said, to find where "your deep gladness and the world's deep hunger meet." There you will find a job, a career, a business, and a life worth living. We cannot talk ourselves into doing something we do not inherently enjoy, no matter how spiritual that something may appear to those around us.

Pastor Bob had resented the resistance of his congregation for years. They seemed slow to act and only moderately supportive of his ideas for growth and change. Their resistance was reflected in their lack of financial support. He had 2 paper routes, requiring him to start each Sunday morning at 3:30 A.M., delivering papers for 3 hours before delivering his message. His wife was working a stressful job to add to their meager income. And yet all this was justified because he was "serving God." His early interest in engineering had been discarded based on an influential person declaring that Bob was *called* to preach. Even with no affirmation in his work, he was still struggling to fulfill that expectation.

What a dismal picture! God does not call us to this kind of Christian living. *Sanctified ignorance* is no excuse for a life out of alignment, lacking joy, fulfillment, and a clear sense of accomplishment. If you are a street sweeper, then do it with joy. The Bible does not rank the godliness of occupations; only modern Christians do that. Look at how God has uniquely gifted you in your skills and abilities, personality traits, and values, dreams, and passions. It is in these that we find the authentic path designed for us for a purpose-driven life.

THE WHEEL OF MY LIFE

Each of the categories in the wheel below represents a portion of our lives. Rate yourself by shading in each section the degree to which you are reaching success in that category. (A score of 10 is great, while a score of 1 puts you at the center of the wheel and means you need some work.)

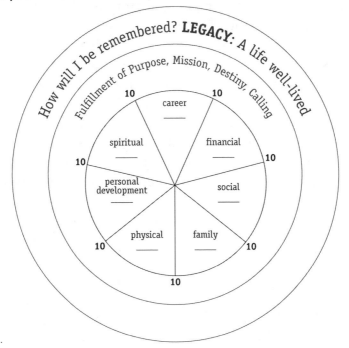

You know what an unbalanced wheel does. An unbalanced life does much the same. No one wants to be in the hospital with a heart attack even if you have $5 million in the bank. And no one wants to be in great physical shape but rejected by family and friends. You cannot justify success in one area at the expense of success in another. Make the decision now to have success in all 7 areas. Learn to recognize when you are making a withdrawal or a deposit physically, spiritually, relationally, etc. Without clearly defined goals in each of these areas, the activities of your life will reflect the desires of those around you.

NEED TO PRAY ABOUT IT
(OR JUST INDECISION)?

Frequently in my life coaching, I notice that people are crippled in life because of indecision. Recently, a gentleman told me that he had been with his company for 17 years and that he had hated his job for 16 years and 11 months. My obvious question was, "Why are you still there?" But the fear of having to make a new decision was just too intimidating for him. Consequently, the indecision kept him going to a job he detested.

A common response from Christians when confronted with any decision is, "I'll need to pray about it." While certainly admirable from a spiritual standpoint, I find this is often nothing but a socially acceptable method of making no decision. Days, weeks, and months go by with unresolved situations and choices. Again, it's insanity to continue doing what you've always done and yet expect different results. Continuing indecision and hiding behind a spiritual smoke screen doesn't lead to different results either.

The workplace today is filled with new and exciting opportunities. Unemployment is at a relative low, and companies are desperately seeking new workers. Twenty-four million Americans have made the decision to start their own businesses. But unhappiness and frustration at work continues even for Christians. There is little explanation for this outside of the lack of clear focus and crippling indecision.

Can you live with the results of your own inaction? Recognize that even making no decision is a decision.

A recent Harvard Business School study asked, "What are the top characteristics of high achievers?" Of course, the list of answers included intelligence, education, and attitude. But at the very top of the list, one characteristic stood out: *speed of implementation*—having the ability to act quickly. Eighty percent of decisions should be made immediately.

Jim Rohn speaks to this issue in his book *Facing the Enemies Within*: "Indecision is the greatest thief of opportunity." Or what about this quote from D. L. Moody: "Every mistake I've made in my life, I made when I thought twice."

The Bible adds its wisdom in James 1:6–8: "But let him ask in faith without doubting. For the doubter is like the surging sea, driven and tossed by the wind. That person should not expect to receive anything from the Lord. An indecisive man is unstable in all his ways."

Indecision is a crippling characteristic. Indecision in one area will carry its negative effects to other areas of life. I have seen parents who are unsure about selecting a school for their child become almost incapable of functioning for months, agonizing over this decision. I have seen frustrated workers who remain in toxic corporate cultures because they are unable to decide to move on. And I have witnessed self-owned businesses slowly fail as the owners feel unable to make the decision to stop their deepening hole.

My wife, Joanne, and I have used a concise process for the 36 years of our marriage. When confronted with a decision, we allow a 2-week maximum for arriving at a decision. Whether it is where to move, what kind of car to purchase, making a career or business decision, or how to handle a difficult relationship with a relative, we approach the process as follows:

1. State the problem.
2. Get the advice and opinions of others.
3. List the alternatives.
4. Choose the best alternative.
5. Act.

Yes, this process must be bathed in prayer. But a daily walk with God should provide confidence in moving ahead quickly with most decisions.

You, too, can deal effectively with the challenge of making solid decisions. Don't be indecisive and unstable in all your ways. Rather, walk in the strength, confidence, and boldness that come from decisive action.

THE POWER OF HAVING A GOAL

Considerable evidence indicates that expectations of your future do, in fact, tend to create your future. Dr. Paul Yonggi Cho, head of the world's largest church, says: "What you have in your heart becomes your experience."

People often end up where they expect to end up.

It seems reasonable to spend some time determining specific, worthwhile expectations that will make your life more meaningful.

"With definite goals you release your own power, and things start happening."
— Zig Ziglar

Keep in mind that only about 8 percent of the general population can identify clear goals and only about 3 percent ever actually write those down. These are specific goals, not just the "I want a bigger house and a nicer car" variety. With this process, you can quickly put yourself into the 3 percent category, noting that those 3 percent ultimately accomplish more than the remaining 97 percent.

Remember, in this career- and life-planning process you will be identifying your:

1. skills and abilities,
2. personality traits,
3. values, dreams, and passions

As you integrate these identified areas into realistic areas of opportunity well suited to you, you will consolidate them into goals. The following process will help you get an initial focus. You may feel you are being rushed or hurried. However, you will find that if you do not begin to make decisions, you will tend to procrastinate and your history will simply repeat itself. A quick decision is often the best decision and is certainly better than no decision. And you might want to be reminded that *insanity* is to keep doing what you've always done and expect different results.

Goals are not written in concrete terms but certainly give you a starting point and a destination. The important thing is that you are working on your goals; your life has meaning only when you are working toward goals through which you achieve your meaning. After all, success is *the progressive realization of worthwhile goals.*

Master Gardener of Your Soul

Our minds are like gardens; they grow whatever we allow to take root.

Just as a gardener cultivates his plot, keeping it free from weeds, and growing the flowers and fruits, which he requires, so may a man tend the garden of his mind, weeding out all the wrong, useless, and impure thoughts, and cultivating toward perfection the flowers and fruits of right, useful, and pure thoughts. By pursuing this process, a man sooner or later discovers that he is the master gardener of his soul, the director of his life. He also reveals, within himself, the laws of thought, and understands, with ever-increasing accuracy, how the thought-forces and mind-elements operate in the shaping of his character, circumstances, and destiny. (James Allen, *As a Man Thinketh*)

Control your own destiny by controlling what goes into your mind. The books you read, the thoughts you think, the television you watch, the conversations you participate in, the people you associate with, and the music you listen to combine to create your future. Are you sowing the seeds for the life you want 5 years from now?

For your purpose in life to be fulfilled, you must set goals in multiple areas. Success is not just career-related or financial; family, physical, and spiritual areas are equally important aspects of achievement. They are part of the same whole. This is the whole-person concept of the *48 Days to the Work You Love* approach.

Time is the only resource you can never recapture. Are you *spending* or *investing* your time? Remember: *A goal is a dream with a timeframe on it.*

Personal Checkup: Where Am I Now?

1. Am I missing anything in my life right now that's important to me? __ YES __ NO
2. I know what I am passionate about. __ YES __ NO
3. I am well organized, know how to focus on my top priorities, and get a lot done every day. __ YES __ NO
4. I have a written, strategic plan for my work and personal life with time lines and quantifiable measurements.
   __ YES __ NO
5. I have ample time for my family and social relationships and feel good about the balance I have achieved.
   __ YES __ NO
6. I exercise 4 to 5 times a week to restore myself physically.
   __ YES __ NO
7. I am regularly achieving my income goals. __ YES __ NO
8. My life reflects my spiritual values and I am growing, maturing, and gaining wisdom in this area. __ YES __ NO
9. I studied and developed the new, creative ideas I had in the past year. __ YES __ NO
10. I believe I am fulfilling my mission in life. __ YES __ NO

. . . .

▶ Living My Dreams

Recently in life coaching a young man, I heard him say, "My fear is that I will discover what I love doing but by then be too old to enjoy a full life of living it out." Wow, what an approach-avoidance conflict. Remember those from your introductory psychology classes? You want a cookie but know that if you reach for it your hand will get slapped.

What about this above stated fear? When do you cross the line age-wise where it's just better not to want or know about a better life, but better to only exist and wait for the grave? Is it 35, 50, or 70? I've had 27-year-olds who are fearful that they've missed the window of opportunity for a life well lived. If your dream was to play quarterback in the Super Bowl, that may be true, but for most of us, living out our dreams is not 1 event.

Look for recurring themes in things that get your attention. Is it art, music, children, the elderly, cars, caring and nurturing, birds, reading, flying? Don't think that your dream needs to be new and revolutionary. We all know someone like Susie who sells seashells by the seashore, but most lives of fulfillment may look ordinary to an observer. We find that even those who end up extremely wealthy are not necessarily doing something rare; rather the critical element is that they are doing something they truly enjoy.

Be confident you can live out your dreams. Don't settle for less!

GOALS

Any stage in life can be an exciting time with many opportunities or a dreary time of confusion and entrapment. You may not be able to change your circumstances, but you can decide that the circumstances won't dominate you. You do have choices.

Something magical happens when you write down your goals. I have seen people transform their levels of success almost instantly simply as a result of getting clearly defined and written goals.

"Begin to weave and God will give the thread."

— *German proverb*

So spend some time determining specific, worthwhile expectations that will make your life more meaningful. If you don't have a written plan for your life, it may feel like you're driving a car without having your hands on the wheel.

On May 6, 1954, Roger Bannister ran the first under-4-minute mile in recorded history. Doctors said it could not be done—that the human heart would explode with such exertion. Six weeks later an Australian runner duplicated that feat. Approximately 1 year later, 8 college runners at 1 track meet all broke the 4-minute mile. What changed? Did humans suddenly evolve to be faster than ever before in history? Not likely. What did happen is that the level of expectation changed. What was believed to be impossible was proven to be possible. Most of us operate under clear beliefs about what we are able to accomplish. If those beliefs are changed, the results change as well.

Zig Ziglar has a famous story about flea training: If you put fleas in a jar with a lid on it, they will desperately pop up against that lid in an attempt to escape for about 20 minutes. Then, while fully convinced they cannot get out of the top of that jar, you can remove the lid. With a perfectly clear path to freedom, those little fleas will starve to death in that jar. They tried escaping once and they *believe* they have no other option. I find many people living their lives within boundaries that exist only in their minds.

> *"The best way to predict your future is to create it."*
> — Stephen Covey

Are you a goal setter? Do you typically set goals at the first of the year? If not, why not? Goals give you a starting point and a destination. It is the easiest way to give meaningful direction to your life, which releases you to effectively use your talents.

Identify 5-year goals then work backward to what you need to do today to make deposits in where you want to be 5 years from now. Be specific, creating quantifiable benchmarks to track your deposits of success. Saying you want to be a better mommy, have a better job, or learn a new language is admirable, but without listing steps of measurable, specific goals, you will not move toward any specific action. Then another year will pass without any real change.

If you can plan out for 5 years from now, you will likely be amazed at how doors start opening. People who cannot see 5 years out ultimately end up feeling like victims of circumstances. They feel like they are being pushed along the railroad of life with a locomotive right behind them.

7 AREAS FOR ACHIEVEMENT

1. *Financial:* income and investments (if you can't dream it, it won't happen). "Take delight in the Lord, and He will give you your heart's desires" (Ps. 37:4).

How much do you want to be earning each year in 5 years?

How much do you want to have in the bank or in investments?

If you can't dream it, it won't happen! Nothing is unrealistic if you have a clear plan.

Don't let failure cripple you. "If thou faint in the day of adversity, thy strength is small" (Prov. 24:10 KJV).

2. *Physical:* health, appearance, and exercise.

Do you take long walks, exercise, or meditate regularly?

Are you living a balanced life? Is this an area that deserves more time?

Can you just give yourself 30 minutes to relax?

Do you know that physical exercise is a cleansing process that can dramatically increase your creativity?

> *"He who cannot
> endure the bad
> will not live to see
> the good."*
>
> — *Old Yiddish proverb*

Wealth is difficult to enjoy if you've given up health in the process.

"Now may the God of peace Himself sanctify you completely. And may your spirit, soul, and body be kept sound and blameless for the coming of our Lord Jesus Christ" (1 Thess. 5:23).

"The feeling of being hurried is not usually the result of living a full life and having no time. It is, on the contrary, born of a vague fear that we are wasting our life. When we do not do the one thing we ought to do, we have no time for anything else—we are the busiest people in the world." — Eric Hoffer

3. *Personal Development:* knowledge, education, and self-improvement.

Your success, financial and otherwise, will never far exceed your personal development. Start doing something that you've put off because of the risk of failure.

Want to learn a new language? Do it this year.

How many books will you read this year? It is said that if you read 3 books on any subject, you will be an expert in that topic.

Take time for personal development, which is the inhaling part of healthy personal breathing—if you do nothing but exhale, you'll turn blue and pass out. Peter Drucker says, "Knowledge by definition makes itself obsolete." The only thing that will allow you to be a leader in today's environment is to be a continuous learner. Don't end your education when you finish high school, college, etc. Why do you think the ceremony is called *commencement?*

> *"Never rest on your achievements; always nurture your potential."*
> — Denis Waitley

(Speaking of time, join the Automobile University—if you drive 25,000 miles a year at an average speed of 46 mph, you will spend about the same amount of time in your car as an average college student spends in the classroom. The question then is, What are you doing with that time? You can listen to tapes and transform your success. See the appendix for audio options.)

Where do you look for inspiration, mentors, and positive input?

What gifts do you have that you have not been using? Is there some potential for full achievement that needs to be unlocked?

"Get wisdom, get understanding;
don't forget or turn away from the words of my mouth.
Don't abandon wisdom, and she will watch over you;
love her, and she will guard you.
Wisdom is supreme—so get wisdom.
And whatever else you get, get understanding."
(Prov. 4:5–7)

4. *Family:* relationship to others, development of children, location of household.

In a speech to graduates of Wellesley College, Barbara Bush said, "Whatever the era, whatever the times, one thing will never change: fathers and mothers, if you have children, they must come first. You must read to your children and you must hug your children and you must love your children. Your success as a family, our success as a society, depends not on what happens in the White House, but on what happens inside your house."

The second law of thermodynamics is things left to themselves tend to deteriorate. Great relationships don't just happen—they come as the result of making deposits toward the "success" you want.

> *"The greatest good you can do for another is not just to share your riches, but to reveal to him his own."*
> — *Benjamin Disraeli*

What is the kind and length of vacation you will take this year? What is your goal for free time with family and friends?

You may try taking the time you normally spend watching a favorite TV show and spend that time instead with your spouse, a child, or a friend.

To be a "better" mom, dad, or parent, define what "better" means. You may decide to spend 20 minutes each night with your child or 1 Saturday morning a month doing what the child wants to do. Or how about scheduling 1 overnight event with your spouse every quarter of the year?

5. *Spiritual:* church involvement, personal commitment, and Scripture study.

"Search me, God, and know my heart;
test me and know my concerns.
See if there is any offensive way in me;
lead me in the everlasting way." (Ps. 139:23–24)

Can you say that you are now living out God's purpose for your life?

What are you a part of that goes beyond yourself?

How have you handled a crisis this last year?

Are you comfortable taking steps of faith, or are you more comfortable with what you have already seen?

Do you trust your dreams as being inspired?

How will you be remembered?

6. *Social:* increased number of friends, community involvement, etc.

Change old attitudes. Discard past negatives. Ask for forgiveness. Make things right with people whom you need to forgive or who need to forgive you.

Choose someone you could care for or be a mentor to, and then make the effort to work on this relationship starting today.

What is a promise you made to someone but failed to keep?

Spend time with an elderly person and find out some of his fondest memories.

Six ways to make people like you:

1. Become genuinely interested in other people.
2. Smile.
3. Remember that a person's name is to that person the sweetest and most important sound in any language.
4. Be a good listener. Encourage others to talk about themselves.
5. Talk in terms of the other person's interests.
6. Make the other person feel important—and do it sincerely.

—from *How to Win Friends and Influence People* by Dale Carnegie

7. *Career:* ambitions, dreams, and hopes.

"Moreover, when God gives any man wealth and possessions, and enables him to enjoy them, to accept his lot and be happy in his work—this is a gift of God" (Eccles. 5:19 NIV).

Your career should be a *reflection* of the LIFE you want; it is an outcome of knowing what you want in the other 6 areas. Once you decide on the life you want, it becomes obvious what kind of work embraces that. We want to help you plan your work around the life you want.

These 7 areas are integrally connected. They can rise up together or spiral down together. That's why if someone has lost a job, I may recommend that as a first step he go for a brisk 3-mile walk each morning. Then spend more time with his spouse and play with his children and volunteer in his church and community. Making immediate deposits of "success" in those areas will speed his success in the struggle.

When a person loses a job, we know the first area to be impacted negatively will be *career.* The next immediate one effected is *financial.* With those two in trouble, *family* relationships are likely to be strained, causing *personal development* and self-esteem to crumble. Naturally, he's embarrassed and doesn't want to hang out with the guys right then (*social*). With all of this negative stress on Monday morning, rather than being out beating the streets, the poor guy is sitting on the couch eating Pringles and watching *Oprah.* So *physically* he begins going to pot—and of course in all of this he wonders, "Why is God angry with me?" (*spiritual*).

> *"It is good to dream, but it is better to dream and work. Faith is mighty, but action with faith is mightier. Desiring is helpful, but work and desire are invincible."*
> — *Thomas R. Gaines*

That's not an uncommon scenario. So how can you reverse or prevent that downward cycle? Several years ago I saw a young man who had lost $3.2 million in 18 months. It was money inherited from his grandmother; unfortunately, he made some bad business investments and got cleaned out. So career-wise and financially he was in the tank. I had him start going to the YMCA each morning. This kept his mind occupied, his energy focused and away from the Pringles and television. He got in such good shape, you could bounce quarters off this guy's chest. I truly believe that the energy and vitality that exploded out of his physical well-being positioned him to very quickly bounce back in the initial areas of lack—which he did.

In 1988 I experienced a major disaster myself. I had leveraged one business into the next and was in a vulnerable position when some banking regulations changed. I ended up losing everything we had financially. Notice I did not say we crashed and burned or that I failed at everything I did, but I did lose all our money. We lost our custom-built house, our cars, and anything else of value that the IRS could track down. I knew I was fertilized for negative thinking to take root and grow quickly.

I borrowed a car from a friend. It was a Mercury Zephyr station wagon. The windows didn't work, the radio was shot, and it used a quart of oil about every 100 miles. But I carried a little portable cassette player with me and started listening to cassettes. I listened to everything I could get my hands on that was positive, pure, clean, and inspirational. I was in the car much of the day and I dedicated at least 2 hours daily to the listening process. I filled all my waking time with positives, leaving little room for the negatives. And I began to experience success in some new areas. I took a job in commissioned sales, experiencing lots of daily rejection but with the quickest income plan I could find.

Those 2 hours daily had such a profound effect on my thinking and success that I have never discontinued it. I discovered the power of the first hour of the day, what Henry Ward Beecher called "the rudder of the day—the golden hour."

Be very careful how you start your morning. You are planting the seeds for what the day will hold. If you get up late, grab a cup of coffee and a cigarette, fume at the idiots in traffic in your rush to work, and drop down exhausted at your desk at 8:10, you have set the tone for your day. Everything will feel like pressure, and your best efforts will be greatly diluted.

However, if you get up leisurely after a completely restful night's sleep, you can choose a different beginning. I have not used an alarm clock for the last 25 years because I go to bed at a reasonable time and have clearly in my mind when I want to start the next day. I get up, spend 30 minutes in meditative and devotional reading, and then go to my workout area. While working out physically, I take advantage of my extensive tape library, so that I fill that 45 minutes with physical exertion combined with mental input and expansion. The motivation of Earl Nightingale, Zig Ziglar, Brian Tracy, Kenneth Blanchard, Jay Abraham, and Denis Waitley; the philosophy of Aristotle and Plato; the theology of Robert Schuller, Dietrich Bonhoeffer, and John Maxwell are the first input into my brain each morning. I never read the paper first thing in the morning, no matter how important it may seem to know the news. The news is filled with rape, murder, pestilence, and heartache, and that is not the input I want in my brain. Later in the day, I can scan the news for anything related to my areas of interest and quickly sort through what I need. But I carefully protect that first hour of the day, making sure that all input is positive, creative, and inspirational. Many of my most creative ideas have come from this protected time of the day, often when I am in a full sweat. By 9:00 A.M. I am invigorated, motivated, and ready to face anything the day may bring.

"Let me experience
Your faithful love in the morning,
for I trust in You.
Reveal to me the way I should go,
because I long for You." (Ps. 143:8)

"Our Careers Kept Us Apart"

I rarely purchase the sensational magazines in the grocery checkout lane but once made an exception. The front cover of *US Weekly* had the headline "Tom and Nicole Separate—'Our Careers Kept Us Apart.'" Give me a break! Do they have to keep their work schedules to make the mortgage payment? No, this is just an extreme example of misplaced priorities! Here's a quote from the article: "Citing the difficulties inherent in divergent careers which constantly keep them apart, they concluded that an amicable separation seemed best for both of them at this time." Yeah, explain that to the 8- and 6-year-old children. "Kids, Mommy and Daddy think having a great career is more important than being a family."

With all the options today, it is critical to define your own priorities. If you simply respond to circumstances, any obstacle will send you in a new direction. Circumstances should not determine our choices. Priorities can guide us through the inevitable changes that will come our way. Careers are tools for successful lives, but nothing more than one piece of a successful life.

From the beginning of this chapter, remember Pastor Jones with his sanctified ignorance? He is redesigning his life as well. The years of moving off track cannot be recaptured completely, but he can redirect to capture the value of his remaining years. He is working in an engineering firm with many opportunities to share his faith and values. His income has increased dramatically, reducing the stress and resentment of his wife and children. He is on a stringent program to reduce his weight and is experiencing the immediate satisfaction of the tiny steps of success. Godly insight and action are replacing his years of *sanctified ignorance*.

COUNTDOWN TO WORK I LOVE

1. Are you a goal setter? Do you typically set goals at the first of the year? If not, why not?
2. How would you describe your current focus on work?
3. What hobbies do you have? What other skills and interests do you have?
4. How are you involved in your community?
5. What was your father's or mother's attitude toward work and how has that affected you?

Am I an Eagle or an Owl?

"A Prayer for Joy"

Help me, O God,
To listen to what it is that makes my heart glad
And to follow where it leads.
May joy, not guilt,
Your voice, not the voices of others,
Your will, not my willfulness,
Be the guides that lead me to my vocation.
Help me to unearth the passions of my heart
That lay buried in my youth.
And help me to go over that ground again and again
Until I can hold in my hands,
Hold and treasure,
Your calling on my life.

—KEN GIRE, *WINDOWS OF THE SOUL*

Ralph Waldo Emerson talked about the concept of "divine discontent," that state of knowing we are not really walking out God's perfect plan for our lives. He continued to say that "the mass of men lead lives of quiet desperation." The popular singing group Sixpence None the Richer has a recent CD titled *Divine Discontent*. It is a thematic expression of our justifiable dissatisfaction with things in this life that are causing dissonance or continued unrest.

Improper matching of our uniqueness and the work we perform each day is a large contributor to this "divine discontent."

Looking at your own uniqueness is a necessary starting point for finding proper career direction. Identifying our inner gifts and talents and using them effectively in our work are critical components of our spiritual well-being.

Therefore, expecting the government or corporations to provide jobs is to reverse the process of finding your own vocation. A true vocation helps us grow as people while we meet our own needs and address the needs of those around us. To have someone *give* you a job is likely to short-circuit the process of finding your calling.

You can structure your work around goals and meaningful relationships and your unique personality, dreams, and passions. Look inward to give shape to the work that is fitting for you, and the application will appear.

Expect change and workplace volatility to enhance your chances of creating meaningful work. It is often in the midst of change and challenges that we find our true direction.

Emerson adds, "A foolish consistency is the hobgoblin of little minds, adored by little statesman and philosophers and divines. With consistency a great soul has simply nothing to do."

The "Humus" in My Life

If you are a backyard gardener, you appreciate the value of humus—the decayed leaves and vegetable matter that feeds the roots of your plants. It's interesting to note that the same root word for *humus* gives rise to the word *humility,* explaining that the "humiliating" events of my life, the events that leave "mud in my face," may be the fertilizer in which something new and great can grow.

Fifteen years ago I crashed and burned in my business. Handshake relationships with the bank changed and my notes were called. I was forced into selling a health and fitness center at auction, resulting in owing more than $100,000 in personal debt. That "humiliating" experience refined my thinking and understanding of business. Today, I am free of bank debt and have a nontraditional business, an incredible sense of meaning and purpose in my work, and far more income than I did back in those days.

Remember, it's usually in the midst of muck and mess that the conditions for rebirth are being created.

Looking inward first is the only realistic way to develop a proper direction outward. I tell people that 85 percent of the process of having the confidence of proper direction is to look inward. Fifteen percent is the application—résumés, interviews, etc. Our society teaches us to put the cart before the horse—to get a job and then make your life work. Wrong! To have real "success" you must understand yourself and plan your life first, then plan your work to embrace the life you want. The principles in *48 Days to the Work You Love* are not just a process of rational analysis or a series of tests to define your abilities. Rather, the principles teach a process of learning to pay attention to what God has already revealed to you—people, events, and activities that evoke the strongest response in you. The process is more intuitive than logical. Our hearts have to join our heads to find true life direction. Career testing has always been artificial and inadequate, looking primarily at abilities. Times of change are great opportunities to pay attention to your heart; to see recurring themes in what you enjoy and are drawn to.

"He who knows others is learned. He who knows himself is wise."
— Lao-Tse

Three Key Areas to Consider

The time spent looking at yourself will provide a 100 percent payback in terms of helping you create a proper direction. The more you know about yourself, the more confidence you can have about choosing the right work environment.

Any job you have must blend the following three personal areas.

SKILLS AND ABILITIES

Yes, you must have the ability to do your job, but keep in mind that skill or ability alone will not necessarily lead to a sense of purpose and fulfillment. You may be an excellent dentist and yet be unfulfilled in doing dentistry. Many people have demonstrated the ability to do something well and yet are miserable in doing it day after day. Keep in mind that most career testing focuses on what you have the *ability* to do. By the time you reach the age of 25 to 30, you probably have the ability to do 150 to 200 different things. Having the ability is not enough reason to spend your time and energy doing something. It has to go beyond that alone.

Skill areas could include marketing, budgeting, computer programming, serving customers, accounting, supervising, counseling, training, writing, organizing, designing, etc.

PERSONALITY TENDENCIES

How do you relate to other people? In what kinds of environments are you most comfortable? Are you a people person, or are you more comfortable with projects and tasks? Are you expressive and visionary, or are you analytical, logical, and detailed? Do you like a predictable environment, or do you seek change, challenge, and variety? Clarification will help you identify the best working situation for yourself.

Unfortunately, success in a position can cause you to be promoted to a position that is not a good fit. The classic book *The Peter Principle,* by Dr. Laurence J. Peter, clarifies how people in our culture are often promoted out of where they function best to a position of incompetence. A bank teller who is loved by her customers may be promoted to branch manager where she has to manage the financial details. A great line worker may be promoted to shift boss, turning him into the disciplinarian with the guys who used to be his friends. A great salesman will be promoted to sales manager where he is expected to oversee the scheduling of the staff's work schedule.

Knowing your strongest personality traits should allow you to stay true to those areas that are authentic and enjoyable.

Common personality traits are grouped into four categories:

1. *Dominance (Driver)—Lion—Eagle:* Takes charge, likes power and authority, confident, very direct, bold, determined, competitive.

2. *Influencing (Expressive)—Otter—Peacock:* Good talkers, outgoing, fun-loving, impulsive, creative, energetic, optimistic, variety-seeking, promoter.

3. *Steadiness (Amiable)—Golden Retriever—Dove:* Loyal, good listener, calm, enjoys routine, sympathetic, patient, understanding, reliable, avoids conflict.

4. *Compliance (Analytical)—Beaver—Owl:* Loves detail, very logical, diplomatic, factual, deliberate, controlled, inquisitive, predictable, resistant to change.

*See my "48 Days Personality Report System & Step-by-Step Personal Application Guide" at: http://www.48days.com/work personality.php

You can complete a short survey and receive your full report immediately; including a list of suggested careers based on your personal style responses. As a bonus you'll receive a "Biblical Character Match" and have access to an audio Step-by-Step Application Guide. This is the same profile I use as a starting point with all of my personal life coaching clients, and we have hundreds of churches and businesses who use these reports for team building and accurate job matching.

> "To live a creative life, we must lose our fear of being wrong."
> — Joseph Chilton Pearce

VALUES, DREAMS, AND PASSIONS

What is it that you find naturally enjoyable? If money were not important, what would you spend your time doing? When do you find the time just flying by? What are those recurring themes that keep coming up in your thinking? What did you enjoy as a child but perhaps have been told was unrealistic or impractical to focus on as a career?

This is a tough area for most people. There is a subtle spiritual myth that following our dreams is selfish, egotistical, and something God would frown on. However, we are created in God's image and as such are creators ourselves. Why would God have created us to think imaginatively and to have vivid dreams only to then squelch those dreams for practicality? Trust your dreams as having come from a divine source. And as you move toward your values, dreams, and passions, you will move toward being more spiritual and more fully what God created you to be.

Dreamers of the Day

In *Seven Pillars of Wisdom,* T. E. Lawrence says, "There are dreamers, but not all human beings dream equally. Some are dreamers of the night, who in the dusty recesses of their mind dream and wake in the morning to find it was just vanity. But the Dreamers of the Day are dangerous people because they act their dreams into reality with open eyes."

In today's sophisticated, technological world we often dismiss our dreams as the result of too much pizza or having too much on our minds when we went to bed. Don't underestimate the value of your night dreams for problem solving and creative approaches to your situation. And by all means, keep dreaming during the day. Tap into those recurring thoughts and ideas that have followed you for years.

If you can't dream it, it won't happen. Success doesn't sneak up on us. It starts as a dream that we combine with a clear plan of action. Become a Dreamer of the Day and watch your success soar.

I find many people have squandered their creative energies by investing largely in the hopes, dreams, plans, and expectations of others. Well-meaning parents, friends, teachers, and pastors may have exerted subtle control to obscure and misdirect your own directions. I frequently find professionals in their 40s and 50s who are discovering that the life they are living is not their own. Wanting encouragement and support is quite natural, and we seek this first from our nuclear family, then from an ever-widening circle of friends and people of influence. Unfortunately, this encouragement seldom supports a really individualized path, but rather the broad applications of "doctor, dentist, teacher, lawyer, plumber, engineer," etc. Caution is the common response to anything radically different, unique, or creative in application. Thus, after adding the fears of friends and family to a person's own, the "safe" path is chosen. And there, caught between exciting dreams and the fear of failure, boring career paths are born.

Thus, the most frequently stated challenge I hear is, "I'm still trying to figure out what I want to be when I grow up." This is often said as an embarrassing self-revelation from a 45-year-old, but it is a healthy and realistic starting point. It's very difficult to see all the options clearly and have the necessary self-understanding at 18 to be able to ask the right questions, much less to be able to make the right choices. Creating proper life direction is an ongoing process—and yes, it can be intimidating and exhilarating at the same time. Value the life experience you have had. Even if unfulfilling and misdirected, it will help provide the clarity by which you can now make really good decisions.

> *"To know what you prefer instead of humbly saying 'Amen' to what the world tells you you ought to prefer, is to have kept your soul alive."*
> — *Robert Louis Stevenson*

Your Self-Esteem Is Slipping

If there is one consistent killer of securing a new job or starting a new business, it's the poor self-esteem of the seeking person.

Here are some telltale signs your self-esteem may be slipping:

- Managing time poorly: You miss appointments or are late for commitments.
- Slacking off on exercise: You take care of what you value, so this is a way of saying, "I don't care about myself."
- Dropping out of group involvement: You say you don't have time this week for school committees, church meetings, study group, etc.
- Becoming a couch potato: You combine what is not urgent with what is unimportant through excessive TV and other pointless, unproductive pursuits.

- Letting relationships deteriorate: You withdraw from nurturing friendships and personal relationships.

Low self-esteem is a common initial outcome of job loss. The cycle is usually one of anger, resentment, unforgiveness, guilt, depression. Depression implies "pressing down energy that wants to be expressed." Depression then leads to more inactivity. Anything that will take you outside of yourself will begin to lessen the cycle. Find a way to be of service and reverse the steps listed above.

MUST EVERYONE FIT THE SAME MOLD?

Frequently, in working on career direction with someone, I realize that person is trying to be in sales when he is skilled in accounting or trying to excel in teaching when she is more gifted in playing music. Why is it that we try to make ourselves something that God has not designed for us? Part of the pressure is that we rank the value of certain jobs or abilities. Would you rather be an average doctor or an excellent carpenter? Would you rather be a mediocre teacher or an outstanding landscaper? I believe we need to carefully identify the special gifts God has given each of us and then be excellent in the use of those gifts.

Let me use a story to illustrate the pressure many of you feel to perform in ways you may not be equipped for. It begins in school.

Once upon a time, all the animals in a special advanced animal kingdom became very excited about the new school that was being formed for all the animal children. Modern administrators organized the school and adopted a curriculum of activities consisting of running, climbing, swimming, and flying.

All the animal parents flocked to the school, eager to enroll their children in this new progressive school. After all, they wanted the very best for their offspring. Mr. and Mrs. Duck enrolled their son, Davy Duck, and expected great things from him because he was an excellent swimmer. In fact, he was better than the instructor. However, Davy had been in school only one week when the administrators discovered that he was quite poor in running, jumping, and climbing trees. So they made him stay after school and practice those skills. Finally, Davy's webbed feet became so badly worn from climbing trees that he then was only average in swimming. But average was acceptable in this school, so no one worried about this except Davy Duck, who really loved swimming.

Now, Ronnie Rabbit was at the top of the class in running but ended up having a nervous breakdown because of having to do so much extra work in swimming. And Sammy Squirrel was excellent in climbing until he developed cramps from overexertion and got a *C* in climbing and a *D* in running.

Ernie Eagle was a problem child and was frequently disciplined. In the climbing class, he beat all the others to the top of the trees, but he did not follow the procedures for climbing and insisted on getting to the top of the tree using his own method. He was not a good team player and often went off on his own. His teachers could not understand his desire to see new things and reprimanded him for daydreaming in the classroom. Ultimately he was put on Ritalin to try to make him a better student.

At the end of the year, Freddie the goldfish could swim exceedingly well and could also run, climb, and fly a little. Freddie had the highest overall score and was voted valedictorian of the class.

The neighborhood dogs stayed out of school and fought the tax levy because the administration would not add digging and fetching to the curriculum. They had noticed the emotional strain on the other students and were considering starting a school of their own.

How sad that we often diminish our best gifts by struggling valiantly to develop in someone else's area of ability. It is better to focus on your uniqueness and do that with excellence than to end up with mediocrity in several areas. Use this rule of thumb for organizing your work strategy:

- Work where you are the strongest 80 percent of the time.
- Work where you are learning 15 percent of the time.
- Work where you are weak 5 percent of the time.

The fulfilling path is usually discovered right under a person's nose. Normally there are recurring themes in life—moments of recognizing being "connected" or "in the zone." In the great old movie *Chariots of Fire,* Eric Liddle is told by his sister to forget his passion for running and to return to the worthy family missionary ministry. I still get goose bumps when I hear Eric reply, "God made me fast, and when I run I feel His pleasure." Don't ignore your true passions even if the normal applications do not seem to produce the income results. A little time spent looking at yourself will provide a big payback in terms of selecting and structuring an opportunity around your unique strengths.

> *"When written in Chinese, the word 'crisis' is composed of two characters—one represents danger, and the other represents opportunity."*
> — *John F. Kennedy*

The integration will be critical and will lead you to recognize clear and consistent patterns, identifying areas of opportunity for career application. Look for the unusual application of your uniqueness. If I say "school teacher," the first thing that comes to mind may be a metro school classroom with 32 kids in the classroom; however, you could be a teacher working for IBM, living in London, England. All you need is one unique application of what integrates your (1) skills and abilities, (2) personality tendencies, and (3) values, dreams, and passions. This is a very individualized process. There is no cookie-cutter plan for everyone, even if there are similarities in background, age, and education.

Risk—Danger or Opportunity?

I frequently hear someone say he would not want to try a new job, a new sport, a new car, or a different route to the office because of the "risk" involved. Certainly, we hear this especially when a person is considering a new career or changing positions. Why leave the predictable for the unpredictable? And yet, that may be the core of the issue. If you go to Las Vegas and put the deed to your house down on a roll of the dice, that's gambling—risking with no reasonable control or plan. However, if you are in a negative work environment and you have checked out your options and are moving to a solid organization with a higher income, how can that be called "risk"? Risk implies jumping off a cliff with no idea what is at the bottom. In business or career moves, we greatly reduce risk by having a careful plan of action. Call it "seizing an opportunity" rather than "risk." Sometimes the greatest risk is not taking one.

DOES MY WORK HAVE ANY MEANING?

Frequently, someone asks me, "Does my work have anything to do with a fulfilling life?" Or "Should I really expect to enjoy my work?"

These questions imply, "Is it just selfish to expect to enjoy my work? Isn't it just part of life to have to work and probably not to enjoy it?" Many of us grew up with a strong American work ethic—we were expected to work on farms or in factories or other labor-intensive businesses without questioning whether it was something we enjoyed. It was our duty. But look at what has happened by adopting that frame of reference. We began to take less pride in the work we were doing, looking forward only to getting to the weekend.

> "Those who loved you and were helped by you will remember you. So carve your name on hearts and not on marble."
>
> — C. H. Spurgeon

This attitude about work has undermined our American society. We do the work because we have to. Thus, we are satisfied with shoddy work, treat customers like impositions, and look for excuses to stay home. Consequently, even as Christians, we have developed a dualistic lifestyle, being Christians on Sunday—concerned about integrity, character, kindness, and goodness—but then the rest of the week, well, that's just work. This compartmentalization won't fly biblically.

The Bible makes no separation of the different areas of our lives—everything is spiritual. "I will praise the LORD at all times" (Ps. 34:1 NLT).

The Bible gives dignity to any work. Any skill God has given you can be used for ministry. Jesus was a stone mason/carpenter. Paul worked with leather goods, and the disciples were fishermen.

Never separate your work from your worship. See what you do during the week as a form of ministry. If you are unable to see your work this way, then you really need to look at changing it. Use the gifts God has given you as a form of ministry just as completely as if you were on the mission field in Africa.

Remember, if you're not in full-time service doing what God has called you to do, for whom are you working?

"My Boss Is Satan's Offspring"

As usual, the rich life stories I hear from people in transition offer colorful phrases. This one came from a young lady in her pre-coaching form: "My company is going in a strictly money-motivated direction, and my manager may very well be Satan's offspring." She further validated her suspicions with lots of examples that certainly convinced me she was accurate.

For your own discernment, here's how to tell if your boss is Satan's offspring. See if these issues are evident in your working environment.

- no morality left
- hatred and fighting
- jealously and anger
- constant effort to get the best for only himself
- complaints and criticisms of everyone except those in the boss's little group
- envy, drunkenness, wild parties

This list is actually a mixture of this lady's stories and another source I refer to frequently. If it sounds a little familiar, you might want to check the list yourself in Galatians 5:19–21.

Fortunately, we also have a list of what to expect with a godly boss:

- love
- joy
- peace
- patience
- kindness
- goodness

- faithfulness   •   gentleness
- self-control

Not too difficult to tell your boss's allegiance, is it?

What special abilities do you have? Frequently, I meet with someone to look at career direction and he says, "I can do anything I put my mind to." In essence, he is saying, "Just give me a job." Do you know how unappealing that attitude is to potential employers?

Employers don't want generalists; they want people who know what their uniqueness is and are looking for opportunities that will allow them to use that uniqueness. Zig Ziglar talks about people whom he calls "wandering generalities," or people who haven't really determined their special abilities.

In a job situation you may be able to learn the skills required, but will that alone give you a sense of accomplishment or meaning? No. You can learn to type, knit, shoot arrows, or do brain surgery, but that doesn't necessarily mean you will be happy doing that. What special abilities has God given you? What special desires has He put in your heart? How do you like to relate to people? Do you enjoy lots of people-contact, or are you more task-oriented? Do you like to create, innovate, and go where no one has gone before, or do you prefer to be part of an established team?

These are all legitimate questions, and it is in the blending of all of these that you can find fulfillment in a job. Rest assured, over the long-term no one is really content just getting a paycheck, no matter how substantial that may be. In addition to the paycheck, we all want a sense of meaning, a feeling of accomplishment to what we do. And what we do vocationally is important; the way we spend 40 to 50 hours a week is no small matter. Our work must be a fulfillment of our unique ministry; otherwise, we are wasting a lot of our time and energy.

The challenge is to develop a clear focus. If you are just looking for a job, that's what you'll get, just a job. I screen hundreds of résumés for companies, and as soon as I detect that the person will do anything, that résumé goes to the bottom of the pile. It's the person who has a clear sense of how God has gifted her with unique skills, abilities, desires, values, and passions who gets called in for an interview.

Don't be misdirected even if you are presented with something that appears more godly, like going overseas or getting involved with a youth ministry or a home for unwed mothers. If God has not gifted you in the things required there, you will be miserable and so will those around you.

Remember 1 Peter 4:10—"Based on the gift they have received, everyone should use it to serve others, as good managers of the varied grace of God." Be thankful for your uniqueness, and get out there and use it for God's glory.

COUNTDOWN TO WORK I LOVE

1. In what kind of settings are you most comfortable?
2. How do you respond to management?
3. How would you manage people?
4. Are you better working with people, things, or ideas?
5. Are you more analytical, detailed, and logical, or are you one to see the big picture and respond with emotion and enthusiasm?
6. Are you steady and predictable, or do you seek variety and new challenges?
7. Are you verbal and persuasive, or are you the caring, empathetic listener?
8. What strengths have others noticed in you?
9. What are 5 words or phrases that describe you?
10. In writing your epitaph, what would you want people to remember about you?

6 Job Offers in 10 Days

There are two kinds of success. One is the very rare kind that comes to the man who has the power to do what no one else has the power to do. That is genius. But the average man who wins what we call success is not a genius. He is a man who has merely the ordinary qualities that he shares with his fellows, but who has developed those ordinary qualities to a more than ordinary degree.

—THEODORE ROOSEVELT

Yes, you must have a résumé. Anyone you approach in your job search is going to want to see a résumé. And even if they did not ask for it, you need the process of creating your résumé. I recommend writing and rewriting your résumé if you currently have a job you love, if you already have a job offer for a new position, if you know Uncle Harry is going to ask you to take over the company, or if you want to start your own business. The process of creating a résumé is one of presenting clearly your strongest areas of competence. In fact, the process of creating your résumé may be more important than the result of that process. You will learn how to tell your story.

I also encourage you to have an "elevator speech." In the time it takes an elevator to go from one floor to the next, you should be able to clearly describe what is unique about you and what you are looking for. The more familiar you are with that speech and the more confident you are that it accurately reflects who you are and what you can offer, the easier it becomes to deliver it with enthusiasm and conviction in a variety of situations.

A résumé is a fresh opportunity to present yourself as a candidate for what you want to do next.

However, regardless of your credentials, your eloquence, and your stunning graphics, a résumé is not going to cause people to stop what they are doing and scream, "This is the person I've been looking for!" Don't get caught up in the fantasy that a "perfect" résumé will get you multiple job offers. A great résumé will get you past the initial screening process and lead to interviews with someone who has the power to hire you. That's all you want it to do.

Getting past this initial screening is not easy, but if you see the whole process, it's certainly possible. Keep in mind that a great résumé provides perhaps 10 percent of the process of an effective job search. In this and the next chapter you will see all the steps in a job search that will help you surpass people with better credentials, experience, and training. Understanding the entire job search process will bring you to offers others will never see.

You do want your résumé to present you as an outstanding candidate for where you want to go. You are not locked into repeating what you have always done. I have helped attorneys, dentists, and pastors redirect their career path by understanding the concept of having "transferable areas of competence."

SHAPING THE OPTIONS

Now that you have looked at yourself, you are ready to begin to look outward at the best options. Only after you have a clear sense of what is unique about YOU can you start to consider the applications that fit you.

As for résumés, I know that in today's competitive workplace you need to stand out, and I am the first to say that a résumé is a place to brag on and embellish accomplishments. However, I am noticing a blurring of embellishment and downright misrepresentation. The rule of thumb seems to be exaggerate and confuse.

Rather than reporting being a greeter at WalMart, people claim to have been a "customer service coordinator for Fortune 500 company." The grease monkey at Jiffy Lube becomes a "petroleum distribution specialist." Yesterday's taxi cab driver appears on the résumé as a "transportation logistics manager." "Engineer for meat inspection and preparation" represents the 18-year-old McDonald's worker.

Keep in mind that today's VP of Personnel was likely a struggling college student herself a few years ago. She probably knows the tricks of the trade, having presented herself as a "human resource specialist" rather than a babysitter.

The bottom line is this: the purpose of a résumé is to help you get an interview. But it plays only one small part in the hiring process. Be prepared to present yourself with confidence and to discuss your ability to contribute.

BUILDING ON THE FOUNDATION

Writing résumés, searching for jobs, interviewing, and negotiating salaries comprise the logistical part of finding the traditional work you love. Now that you have laid the proper foundation, we can look at these important details. Many people see the résumé as the most important part of the hiring process, believing that companies make hiring decisions from them. A company would be foolish to make a hiring decision from a résumé. You don't want your résumé to tell the company enough to make an intelligent decision about hiring you. All you want it to do is whet the interviewer's appetite so that he wants to see you personally. It is in the interview that the rubber meets the road. Everything else is preliminary.

Your résumé is your sales tool for where you want to go. Don't let it be just a snapshot of where you have been. That may or may not be advantageous for you. Recently, I worked with a gentleman who had managed drugstores for years. In that position, and accurately reflected on his résumé, his primary responsibilities were hiring, training, and supervising employees. Guess what he hated more than anything? Hiring, training, and supervising employees. Why would we present him and position him in a way designed to duplicate those duties? We restructured his résumé to show areas of competence like administration, planning, and operations. These were proven abilities of his and allowed him to present himself as a candidate for something much more behind the scenes with less people contact—aspects far more suited to his personality style.

If you want to redirect your career path, you can begin the process with a well-designed résumé. Remember, if your résumé is just a chronological history of what you've done, it will pigeonhole you into continuing to do what you've always done. You can redirect in major ways by identifying "areas of competence" that would have applications in new companies, industries, and professions.

Knowing how to conduct your job search process will transform the results you can expect. Many people become convinced that they are not pretty enough, do not have the right degrees, are too old or too young, or are getting a bad reference from a former employer. How you conduct the job search process will have far more to do with your success than any of those factors.

We are also going to look at how to find the "hidden" job opportunities. We know that only about 12 percent of jobs ever appear in the newspaper, on the Internet, or in another form of advertising. You can find those unadvertised positions and drastically reduce the competition you face for them.

Even though we know that the average job is now only 3.2 years in length, most people remain unprepared for the interview process. They believe that they can send out their résumé, have some company decide it has to have them, and simply show up for a routine interview. Few things could be further from the truth.

The interview is critical. This is where you sell yourself and negotiate the most desirable position. Time spent in preparation and practice will be a great investment.

Knowing that most hiring decisions are made in the first 3 to 5 minutes of an interview confirms that the interviewer is not looking at the fine print on the fourth page of your résumé, but rather is asking herself:

- Do I like this person?
- Will Dan fit in well with the team?
- Is Dan honest?
- Is Dan fun to be around?

These questions are probably going through the interviewer's mind in those first few critical seconds. Be careful of resting on your academic credentials and work experience. Companies realize that they hire a whole person not only a set of definable skills. Remember, you are there to *sell* yourself as the best candidate.

Just Give Me That Job!

No matter how banal, backbreaking, or demeaning a job might be, someone can be found to do it. At least that's what an informal poll by Express Personnel Services has found. The Oklahoma City-based employment firm has hired temporary workers willing to wipe blood and other body fluids from Plexiglas at hockey games for $7 an hour, chase deer off an airport runway for $8 an hour, and pour thousands of cans of rancid beer down a drain for $6 an hour. And here's a couch potato's dream position: getting paid $11 an hour to appear to be working. Express said a company in Redmond, Washington, actually hired 3 temps to look busy and professional to make visitors think it had a larger staff.

While doing my graduate work in clinical psychology, I reviewed some interesting studies. In one experiment, people were hired to dig a trench, put the dirt back in, then move over 2 feet and repeat the process. Although the pay continued to be substantially raised, after about a week, all the workers quit. They would not do what was obviously meaningless work.

I tell people all the time that money is ultimately not enough compensation for investing your time and energy: there has to be a sense of purpose, meaning, and fulfillment.

REAL PREDICTORS OF SUCCESS

So with all the options and opportunities for jobs, what are the real predictors of success? Isn't *ability* still the best predictor of success?

In *48 Days to Creative Income,* I address the 5 predictors of success as:

1. *Passion.* A person with passion is a person who can set goals. Without them, you can have no clear direction and will drift along the road of circumstances.

2. *Determination.* Without a clear purpose, any obstacle will send a person in a new direction. Without determination, you will easily be lured away from your path.

3. *Talent.* No one has talent in every area, but everyone has talent. Discover where you rise to the top. What are those things you love to do whether or not you get paid?

4. *Self-discipline.* Without self-discipline, a person can easily be swayed by others. Self-discipline is the foundation that makes the others work.

5. *Faith.* Even with everything lining up logically, there still comes that step of faith into the unknown. You cannot reach new lands if you keep one foot on the shore.

Unemployment—What's That?

Do you know that in the Tibetan language there is no word for unemployment? That is a concept reserved for our Western culture where we have jobs. In traditional Tibetan society, people were mostly farmers, animal herders, or merchants. There was no concept of set hours of work or of having a job. Their work was often seasonal and during harvest season, they would work very hard. Then during the off-season, they and the land would rest.

That pattern of natural work and rest has been replaced in our culture with 24/7 accessibility to work. Cell phones ring in church, e-mail arrives at 2:00 A.M., demanding a response, and faxes peel off pages of urgent business in family kitchens. We have created artificial environments with artificial work expectations.

I guess that's why I look back and value being raised on a farm where the sun and rain often dictated the day's activities. I love the convenience of modern technology, but, as with all advancements, it brings the responsibility for maintaining personal life balance.

I have always encouraged people to recognize times of being "between opportunities." Rather than the panic of being "unemployed," perhaps we should see those times as welcome times of restoration, rejuvenation, and opportunities for new perspective. Seeing it as such would certainly require a new word. Any ideas?

Résumé Myths

Consider the following myths and beware.

Myth 1: A Good Résumé and Cover Letter Will Get Me the Job

I wish it were that simple. Résumés and letters do not get jobs; they advertise for interviews. A résumé should not tell enough to make a hiring decision. It should simply entice the reader to want to see you. A good résumé will be easy to read and will quickly convey the value of your accomplishments. See it as a sales brochure—like one telling you about a new La-Z-Boy recliner. Did it make you want to go see it and sit in that soft leather, leaning back to let all your stress diminish? That's the same effect you want your résumé to have on the reader.

- Keep typeface simple. Stay away from fancy fonts and graphics—save that for your wedding invitations.
- Present your information in short, easy-to-read paragraphs. Feel free to use bullet points rather than complete sentences.
- Make sure there are no grammatical errors or misspellings.
- Be specific—state that you increased revenues in your territory from $3 million to $5.3 million in a 3-year period or that you reduced office expenses by 13 percent in your first year.

- Don't lie. Be careful about describing yourself as a purchasing manager when you actually picked up the weekly pizza. Don't list yourself as a vice president only because you know that company is no longer in business and there is no way to check on it. And be honest with your credentials. The most lied about item on résumés today is the addition of a nonexistent MBA. Academic degrees are seldom checked and people sometimes fall prey to the temptation to get that extra edge. Don't even think about it. Focus on your areas of competence to make you a top candidate.

Myth 2: The Candidate with the Best Education, Skills, and Experience Will Always Get the Position

Many factors are considered in a hiring decision. Education, skills, age, and ability are only a few of the hiring criteria. Employers interview because they want to see you—how you look, interact, and fit in with their organization.

A recent Yale University study reported that 15 percent of the reason for a person's success is due to technical skill and knowledge, and 85 percent of the reason originates from that person's personal skill: attitude, enthusiasm, self-discipline, desire, and ambition.

This is why candidates with the best qualifications on paper frequently do not get the job. We have been sold the myth that a degree is the magic guarantee for fame and fortune. Not in today's workplace. There are plenty of English literature graduates waiting tables and MBAs mowing lawns. Just be realistic about the importance of a degree in your field of interest. Even in high-level positions, your personal characteristics may outweigh the importance of your degrees. Michael Dell, Bill Gates, Ted Turner, Maya Angelou, Michelle Pfeiffer, and Richard Branson are all college dropouts and yet have achieved high levels of responsibility.

Myth 3: Getting a Job Is Really a Matter of Who You Know or Being in the Right Place at the Right Time

Luck is what happens to people who have clear goals and detailed plans of action. Or luck is when preparation meets opportunity. Don't wait on being in the right place at the right time. Create the situation and the circumstances to make you a candidate for the best positions anywhere. You don't have to know the right people—you just have to get yourself in front of the right people. If you do the right things you will be amazed at how lucky you will become.

Myth 4: Employers Appreciate Long Résumés Because More Information Saves Time Spent Interviewing

Most résumés get a 30- to 40-second look. You must be able to communicate clearly in that time your areas of competence. There is no hard and fast rule about having to stay on 1 page, but there is seldom a reason to go beyond 2 pages in length. The key is to communicate what has value in positioning you as a top candidate. Include only those things that work in creating the image you want to convey. This is not a historical document but a sales brochure. I have a résumé in my file that is 15 pages long. The writer has a Ph.D. in chemistry and listed every study she had ever been a part of. Interesting reading but way too much information.

Myth 5: Always Put Your Salary Requirements and History on Your Résumé

This can only work against you. Whether high or low, it has no positive purpose on a résumé. Salary is to be negotiated after the employer decides you are the right person for the job. Only when an employer wants you and you want them is it appropriate to discuss compensation. Anything prior to that will work against you.

Just think about this. If you are applying for a $76,000 position and in your last position you made $41,000, you will be seen as too low a candidate. Similarly, if you made $92,000 in your last position, they may be reluctant to interview you. Keep in mind that compensation packages are very fluid. If you are the candidate they want, the company may easily find another $10,000 to bring you on board. But if you don't get the opportunity to interview, you will miss even having the chance to discuss your benefits to the company.

MYTH 6: ALWAYS CLOSE A COVER LETTER WITH "I LOOK FORWARD TO HEARING FROM YOU"

Never! Even in times of low unemployment, expecting the receiver to take the initiative is unrealistic. Remember, you must always take the initiative. State when you will call to follow up: "I will call you Thursday morning concerning any questions we both may have and to discuss a personal meeting."

This may appear to be pushy or assertive, and it may be. But what you want is action. Persistence pays. To get the best positions, you will need to stay in the driver's seat in this entire process. No one cares about your success more than you do and no one can present you better than you can. You will need to take the initiative in getting in front of the people who have the ability to hire you. Remember, you have a product to sell and that product is you. The more you approach this process with that mindset, the quicker and better the results will be.

MYTH 7: THE MORE RÉSUMÉS YOU SEND, THE MORE YOU INCREASE YOUR CHANCES OF GETTING A JOB

Not necessarily. Thirty to 40 résumés combined with quality introduction letters, cover letters, and follow-up phone calls are much more effective than 1,000 résumés sent out alone. The Internet makes it so tempting to just send out a million electronic résumés with the push of a button and hope that the law of numbers will work in your favor. That process may be true for playing the lottery, but it is unlikely to work in finding a desirable position for yourself. Well-targeted résumés directed to the right decision makers still get results.

MYTH 8: ONCE YOU SEND YOUR RÉSUMÉ, ALL YOU CAN DO IS WAIT

If you take no action, you will likely get no results. Always follow up by phone. Sending résumés without following up is probably a waste of your time.

But just a minute—isn't waiting a spiritual approach to having God open a door? Of course it is. But I see too many people do too much waiting—wringing their hands, sitting at home, waiting for the phone to ring—and too little working in this process. Isaiah 40:31 says, "But they that wait upon the LORD shall renew their strength; they shall mount up with wings as eagles; they shall run, and not be weary; and they shall walk, and not faint" (KJV). There you go—waiting is scriptural. But if we look at the word *wait* in this context we find that it comes from the same word from which we get *waiter.* Thus a more accurate rendering may be to be doing what an effective waiter would be doing—serving and acting based on what they know needs to be done.

"You can do anything if you have enthusiasm. Enthusiasm is the yeast that makes your hopes rise to the stars. Enthusiasm is the spark in your eye, the swing in your gait, the grip of your hand, the irresistible surge of your will and your energy to execute your ideas. Enthusiasts are fighters, they have fortitude, they have staying qualities. Enthusiasm is at the bottom of all progress! With it, there is accomplishment. Without it, there are only alibis." — Henry Ford

Résumé "Objectives" and Other Ways to Waste Your Time

Here is a recent "objective" on a résumé submitted for my review:

"To support the growth and profitability of an organization that provides challenge, encourages advancement, and rewards achievement with the opportunity to utilize my experience, skills, and proven abilities."

Would you hire this person? But what do you know about this person? Is he a candidate for flipping hamburgers or for a CEO position? Does he have skills in supervising, organizing, planning, selling, marketing, etc? Is he proficient in any computer skills? You don't know. This "objective" tells you absolutely nothing about the person. It was a total waste of time on the applicant's part.

Knowing that most résumés get a 30- to 40-second viewing, you'd better tell the recipient something about yourself that would make him want to see you as a candidate immediately. Begin your résumé with a skills summary, profile, or expertise. Here's an example:

Skills Summary: Over 14 solid years in technology planning and management. Experienced in strategic systems and organizing and overseeing projects. Knowledgeable in R&D, product development, and financial management. Team player in maintaining company policies and procedures. Expertise with IT businesses, especially those with complex technical, logistical, and implementation challenges.

Don't waste your time with generic lead-ins that get you sent to the bottom of the pile. Use your 30 seconds to convey your unique value.

DESIGNING A RÉSUMÉ

Build your résumé so it becomes a sales tool for getting you the position you want. You can present yourself as a top candidate for sales and marketing, administration, organization, developing, training—or whatever your dream position is—if you draw from your experience and identify it in an advantageous way. Let's get started.

Your transferable skills are the most basic unit of whatever career you choose. Once you have mastered a skill in one career, you can transfer that skill to another field and to another career. These skills can also be rearranged, if desired, in a way that opens up a new and different career. Use descriptive terms such as managed, supervised, instructed, planned, organized, trained, directed, edited, recruited, wrote, sold, marketed, created, etc.

The higher your transferable skills, the less competition you face for whatever job you are seeking. Keep in mind that jobs using higher skills are more challenging to find because they are rarely advertised through traditional methods. But the more you understand your areas of competence, the easier it becomes to target those organizations where there could be a potential match.

You always want to claim the highest skills possible. The résumé is the place to brag on yourself; don't be modest. As already mentioned, don't misrepresent yourself, just be bold about how competent you are.

Be specific. If you are reliable, doing what is expected of you and showing up for work on time, you can get any entry-level job today. But as good as they are, those characteristics do little to separate you from everyone else out there. The more specific you can be about what makes you unique, the fewer the competitors and the more you can move up the financial ladder. This may appear to be an irony in a workplace where it appears you must be a jack-of-all-trades. But the reality is that you still need to be able to show unique "areas of competence" to separate yourself from the masses.

There is not one right format for creating a résumé. If you have had increasing levels of responsibility and want to continue in that industry, a straight chronological format may be the best one for you. If you want to redirect your career, then a more functional format will help you. A combination of both chronological and functional is very common and can work well for most people today. The combination résumé is certainly the best choice if you:

- want to change careers and your most recent position has little relationship to what you would really like to do,
- have been a job-hopper with little consistency in the kinds of positions you have had,

- have areas of competence that are part of a position you held several years ago, or
- are reentering the workforce after a lengthy absence.

But I Don't Want to Be a Dentist

Before he became a famous painter, Paul Gauguin worked in a bank. Novelist Tom Clancy started out as an insurance agent. Paul Newman was a construction worker. And many ordinary folks have made the switch from teacher to stockbroker, attorney to franchise owner, pastor to consultant, or dentist to marketing expert.

With people living and working longer, the careers we chose at 20 don't necessarily fit us 2 and 3 decades later. With the volatile changes in medicine, banking, and education, many are taking a fresh look at new, more fulfilling career options.

You can change careers and still embrace your vocation or mission. Again, just be sure to integrate your skills and abilities, personality tendencies, values, dreams, and passions.

These should provide a sense of continuity even if you are changing careers. Use this to create a clear focus. Don't be misdirected just because you hear there will be new job opportunities in a certain area. If the new opportunity does not fit you properly, you will still be frustrated in another 3 to 5 years.

You should cover at least 10 years in your work experience—longer if there is some specific experience that strengthens your presentation. Don't worry if you are just starting into the workforce; draw from areas of competence that you have proven in your school, church, or community. If you have been a housewife for 18 years, don't present yourself as if you have never had a job. Instead, describe your competencies in planning, budgeting, supervising, coordinating events, fundraising, promoting, etc. If you are a high school student, describe your abilities in customer service, delivery accuracy, reliability, graphic design, or Internet savvy.

Having multiple jobs is no longer the red flag it once was. Companies realize that to advance, you may have to move on.

They also realize that in today's volatile workplace, good people are frequently let go through no fault of their own. But you don't have to list every position that you held for a very short time. Also, feel free to list only years rather than months on your résumé to draw attention away from the short length of some positions.

Is Job-Hopping Still a Liability?

Changing jobs early and often isn't the liability it once was, says Allen Salikof, president and CEO of Management Recruiters International Inc. It might even be a plus. Traditionally, employers who saw a job-hopping pattern on a résumé would pass on that candidate in favor of one with more staying power. But job-hopping isn't necessarily the kiss of death anymore, says Salikof. Employers actually favor candidates who have moved around. Some employers are even put off by candidates who have stayed too long in one job or one company where their skills, particularly technological skills, have not had to keep pace with the marketplace.

"If the candidate's history shows consistent increases in salary and responsibility," Salikof says, "job-hopping may tag him or her as a hot property." In some industries you may have to explain why you stayed around so long. Talk about a reversal in traditional thinking!

As for things not to put in a résumé, here are excerpts from actual résumés collected by Robert Half and appearing in a monthly column called "Resumania" for the *National Business Employment Weekly:*

- "An obsession for detail; I like to make sure I cross my i's and dot my t's."
- "Note: Keep this résumé on top of the stack. Use all the others to heat your house."
- "Referees available on request."
- "Work experience: Dealing with customers' conflicts that arouse."

- "My experience in horticulture is well-rooted."
- "Experience with LBM-compatible computers."
- "I have an excellent track record, although I am not a horse."
- "I am a rabid typist."
- "Proven ability to track down and correct erors."
- "Don't take the comments of my former employer too seriously; they were unappreciative beggars and slave drivers."
- "I am loyal to my employer at all costs. Please feel free to respond to my résumé on my office voice mail."
- "Work history: Unsuccessfully searched for a job, incompletion of graduate program, took Bar exam and failed."
- Cover letter: "I've updated my résumé so it's more appalling to employers."
- "My compensation should be at least equal to my age."
- "Experienced in all faucets of accounting."
- "Worked party-time as an office assistant."
- "Work history: Left job because disciplinary actions were taken for showing up late."

BAD REFERENCES

What if you really don't get along with your current boss? Is leaving out of the question because any new employer will have to talk with Mr. Idiot in checking your references?

Well, for starters, it is fairly uncommon for a new employer to talk with your past boss. Don't list him as a reference. Are there others in the company you could ask for a reference? What about that project you worked on last year. Can you use the team leader as a reference? Do you have a former boss who will sing your praises? Do you have customers who will speak well of their relationship with you? How about people you've worked with as a volunteer? Church and community activities are legitimate sources of referrals. Do you have a former professor who believes in you?

And be realistic about the part that references play in your getting that great position: calling references is usually done after the decision has been made to hire you. No one will waste time calling references unless they have already emotionally decided you are the person for the position. Because of the career coaching I do, I am frequently listed as a reference. I don't get three calls a year from prospective employers. With today's job market, few employers even do the checking they should do. And if you want to make sure your references are solidly reliable, try www.jobreference.com.

One word of caution: If you are asked about your current boss, be prepared to put a positive spin on what actually occurred. Don't say anything negative about him or her. And don't say anymore than you are asked.

You will find some examples of real résumés in the appendix. You will see that there are different formats, depending on the purpose of each résumé. Remember, the résumé is only your selling tool in an attempt to get an interview.

Feel free to use as much from the examples as you want. You can copy phrases that apply to your situation, but do personalize your résumé for yourself. Everything in it should work for you. If a piece of information does not help position you as a candidate for what you want to do, don't emphasize or draw attention to it.

Now you are ready to construct or revise your own résumé. Don't make this process more complex than it needs to be. Spend 1 to 2 hours and complete it. Yes, it needs to be great, but it's still only 15 percent of the process. Your creative job search, introduction letters, cover letters, phone follow-up, and interviewing skills are equally important components. Create your own look or choose one of the résumé templates found on any word processing system.

Education—What Is It?

I continue to receive a barrage of e-mail containing concerns regarding education. "I'm 27, have a degree in psychology, and still don't know what I want to do." "My son has dropped out of college and I'm concerned he's on a road to nowhere." "I'm an attorney, four years out of law school, and think I have made a mistake."

What is education? Is our traditional thinking about getting degrees still accurate? *Webster's* dictionary defines *education* as "the process of training and developing the knowledge, skill, mind, and character" of a person. With this definition we can readily see that education can occur in many ways and is certainly not confined to traditional classroom.

I have spent much of my life involved in the academic world, having completed my bachelor's, master's, and doctor's degrees. And yet I have been concerned about the overselling of that kind of education in our country. We know that 10 years after graduation, 80 percent of college graduates are working in something totally unrelated to their college degree. And most of our actors, performers, and business owners have not found college to be their key to success. There are 2 reasons to go to school: (1) to get a piece of paper so someone will give you a job, and (2) for the personal development that takes place.

If you go for the first reason only, you will probably be disappointed. The second can never be taken away. But recognize where personal development can take place. You may work on a construction crew, an organic farm, a day-care, or in a classroom, and all are legitimate places for growth and education.

COUNTDOWN TO WORK I LOVE

1. Do you understand your areas of competence?
2. Do you feel trapped because of your current or past work experience?
3. Do you recognize how easily your abilities may transfer to a new industry or profession?
4. Can you see value in those things you may have done as a volunteer through your church or community?
5. Are there skills or training you need to make you a candidate for the work you love?
6. Has God given you abilities that do not match your desires? If so, how can you reconcile those?

Finding Your Unique Path

Two roads diverged in a yellow wood,
And sorry I could not travel both
And be one traveler, long I stood
And looked down one as far as I could
To where it bent in the undergrowth;
Then took the other, as just as fair,
And having perhaps the better claim,
Because it was grassy and wanted wear;
Though as for that, the passing there
Had worn them really about the same,
And both that morning equally lay
In leaves no step had trodden back.
Oh, I marked the first for another day!
Yet knowing how way leads on to way,
I doubted if I should ever come back.
I shall be telling this with a sigh
Somewhere ages and ages hence:
Two roads diverged in a wood, and I,
I took the one less traveled by,
And that has made all the difference.

—ROBERT FROST, "THE ROAD NOT TAKEN"

Perhaps you are like many others who are employed but wondering if there is a better opportunity out there. Or maybe you are already "between opportunities" and ready to make the next commitment. Searching in today's work environment is much different from what it was even a few years ago.

Keep in mind the transition we have had from "production work" to "knowledge work." If you show up for work and take your place on an assembly line making lunch pails, you are likely to be involved in production work. When you go home at night, the conveyor belts, the machines, the inventory of parts and partially completed lunch pails will stay in the company's buildings. Thus, your means of production stays with them.

But if you are in accounting, data processing, sales and marketing, customer service, computer networking, writing, editing, financial analysis, or a host of other similar functions, then at night you take your means of production home with you. Your tools of the trade are largely between your 2 ears. Thus your skills are much more transferable than those of production workers. Also, look at how knowledge work improves with age and maturity. If you are laying railroad ties, your ability to perform as a production worker may begin to diminish at about age 35. If you are a knowledge worker, you may continue to increase your options, skills, and marketability well into your 70s or 80s.

Over-50 Workers—Sick More Often?

This is only 1 of the myths about older workers. According to the American Council of Life Insurance, workers 45 and older call in sick an average of 3.1 days per year compared to an average of 3.8 days for those 17 to 44.

Bonne Bell Cosmetics in Westlake, Ohio, has a production facility with team members between the ages of 55 and 92. They run 2 4-hour shifts 5 days a week. Bell has found employees they describe as "hard-working, efficient, punctual, and spirited."

The opportunities for older workers are growing daily. The myths that if you are over 50 the opportunities are gone are just not true. And it's not just about WalMart greeters or hamburger flippers. My dad, now 90, drove the Amish to weddings, funerals, etc. after his "retirement" until he was 86 for $1 a mile. How cool for an 86-year-old guy to hang out with friends of similar heritage and make $400 to 500 a day. Here are some additional resources on this growing trend: Administration on Aging (www.aoa.gov), AARP (www.aarp.org), Second Half Strategies

(www.secondhalf.net), Informed Eldercare Decisions, Inc.
(www.elderlifeplanning.com).

Yes, the jobs are changing. Methods of finding new opportunities are changing as well. No longer can you pick up the Sunday
paper, see that your local hardware store is hiring, go down on
Monday morning and see your uncle Fred to get your next job.
The volatility, uncertainty, and transportability of knowledge-
worker skills have put millions of people into the job search.
Knowing that the average job is only 3.2 years in length, even
those who are currently employed are looking for the next position. Because of that, the job you see advertised in the paper will
also be seen by about 3,000 other fully qualified people who may
also be viable candidates.

WHERE JOB LEADS COME FROM

So how do we make sense of this situation, and how do we
find the best fit? The most effective job-hunting method is this:
know your skills, research the potential companies that use those
skills, arrange to see the person who has the power to hire you,
and request the interview. This method, faithfully followed, leads
to a job for 86 out of every 100 job hunters who use it.

Compare that method to the following options:

*Answering local newspaper ads leads to jobs for about 8 out of
100.* (The higher the level of the job you seek, the less effective this
method is.) Understand why this is so ineffective. First, there is a
time lag for the job to even appear in the paper. If it is already common knowledge that a person is needed, current employees may
have already recommended someone who is being hired. It is not
uncommon for the hiring decision to have been made before the ad
ever appears in the paper. Second, companies always look for ways
to find qualified hires without having to go through the process of
screening hundreds of new applicants. So to be run as an ad in the
paper may indicate that current employees are not recommending
the position to those they know (which may say something

negative about the open position). And third, what you see, thousands of others see as well. If it really is a desirable position, they may receive 200 to 300 responses, making it very difficult for your résumé to stand out. The odds are against you. Fourth, many of the newspaper ads are *blind ads,* meaning you can't really tell what the job is or who the company is. Recruiters run these blind ads just to stir up prospects without having real positions available. Many companies run blind ads just to keep a reservoir of candidates. And some companies run blind ads to see if their own employees are looking for new opportunities. If you are spending more than 10 percent of your time using this method, you are wasting time and energy that should be spent in more productive areas.

Private employment agencies and headhunter pursuits lead to jobs for 4 to 22 out of 100. (Again, depending on the level sought. The higher the level, the lower the likelihood of success.) No one can present you as well as you can or cares about your situation as much as you do. I get lots of questions about this process. The bottom line is this: you cannot delegate an effective job search. Don't even think about registering with a couple of employment agencies and then sitting at home waiting for the phone to ring. You could still be sitting there 6 months from now. You must stay in the driver's seat in this entire process.

Answering ads in trade journals leads to jobs for 7 out of 100. (Too much time delay, etc.) I have plenty of horror stories about the selection process in these high-level sounding positions. While at her job as a recruiter at a bank, a young lady responded to a nationally promoted position for a university placement director. They had 386 respondents that they narrowed down to 8. She was one of the 8 who were then scheduled individually for an all-day interview process, including lunch with the university president and his wife. From that process, they narrowed the field to 3. Be aware that this process took place over an 8-month period. My client had already emotionally left her then current position, recognizing her fit for and excitement about this new position. The university then made their selection, not choosing this lady I referenced. I happened to run into one of the committee members soon thereafter and asked how they could possibly have had a candidate superior to my client. He readily agreed that she was by far the best candidate, however, that hiring decision had been made prior to running that original recruiting ad. It was yet one more case of someone's cousin, aunt, best friend's niece, etc. where there was not really an objective selection process in place. They simply went through the motions to satisfy the appearance of equality. My client, reeling from disappointment, quit her current job and went back to her home town.

Fewer than 1 percent of job seekers actually get a position from responding to an Internet ad. (Most people using the Internet as their primary job search tool are simply hiding out, avoiding real contact, and wasting time.) The ads at Monster.com or HotJobs.com look so perfect to you. Just keep in mind that whatever you see, thousands of other great candidates see as well. While there are exceptions to everything, the results here are pretty dismal. A high percentage of companies who have hired from the Internet report a negative experience. We are seeing a pendulum swing back to what we call "behavioral interviewing," where they really want to see you, talk to you, and eat lunch with you. Plus, recognize that if you are responding to ads on the Internet, you are looking at possibilities all over the world—not exactly the way to embrace personal and family priorities as a significant part of a life plan.

790,000 Résumés—And You Think Yours Will Be Seen?

Federal rules requiring many companies to keep job applicant data for a year or more are creating hassles for employers inundated with online résumés.

"It's a huge issue for companies, and it's a hot button," says Barbara Murphy, a spokeswoman at Boeing, which received 790,000 résumés last year.

But critics say the rules set up in the 1970s don't work in the Internet age because it's difficult to know the race of faceless online applicants and keeping résumés doesn't make good sense.

Just be aware that the passive system of sending out
résumés via e-mail or fax has never worked well as part of a professional job search. It's an easy way to stay busy and not get
results.

Better methods for finding a job are available to you.

*Applying directly to an employer without doing any home-
work leads to a job for 47 out of 100.* Just walking in the door,
unannounced, works almost half the time. Notice, this is the second most effective method but works best for lower-level positions. If you want a job at Taco Bell, WalMart, Home Depot, or
Papa John's, don't waste your time with a fancy job search. Just
walk in the door and present yourself as ready to go. I often recommend something similar as part of a transition plan even for
professionals. It's not uncommon for a person to be hired on the
spot in these kind of positions.

*Asking friends for job leads gets a job for 34 out of 100 who
try it.* Don't be hesitant about letting others know what you are
looking for. In sales, we talk about the "3-foot rule." That means
that anytime you get within 3 feet of someone, you tell them what
you are selling. If you're looking for a job, you have a product to
sell, and that product is you. So anytime you get within 3 feet of
someone, tell them about that product. It doesn't have to be a
whining, help-me-out kind of telling. You can ask for their advice
or opinion. Ask what they would do in your situation or how they
would recommend finding a match for your skills.

*Asking relatives for job leads gets a job for about 27 out of
100 who use it.* Yes, even the family system is not a bad source for
finding new opportunities.

*Using the placement office at the school or college you attended
leads to a job for 21 out of 100 who try it.* Colleges and universities recognize that finding a position is not a one-time event.
Graduates are coming back 18 months or 3 years later or longer.

Knowing how to do a great job search will serve you repeatedly over the course of your working lifetime.

The old rule of thumb is that the job-hunt process takes 30 days for every $10,000 of compensation. Thus, a $60,000 position will take 6 months. This is a discouraging statistic, but look at the figures that lead to such a generality. Most people in a job search are contacting 4 to 5 companies a month. At this rate of contact, yes, it may take 6 months. However, finding a position is a sales process and if you understand the numbers involved, you can dramatically increase your rate of success.

The major difference between successful and unsuccessful job hunters is not skill, education, age, or ability, but the way they go about their job hunt. (Perhaps the most important statement in this book!)

If you are selling vacuum cleaners, you may know from the company history that 1 out of 23 contacts will lead to a sale. So then you can decide whether you will make those 23 contacts today or if you will make 1 contact each of the next 23 days. Your rate of making those contacts will determine the timing of your success. Keep in mind that your job search is much the same process. What I lay out here is a short 30-day burst of focused activity, leading to whatever level of compensation you desire in a much shorter period of time.

Two-thirds of all job hunters spend 5 hours or less on their job hunt each week, according to the U.S. Census Bureau. If you are serious about seeking a new position, you cannot afford this rate of progress. My advice, based on seeing successful job hunters, is to spend 35 hours per week in the search. This will dramatically cut down the time in weeks and months to conduct a successful search.

"Low Wages, Long Hours"
"Men wanted for hazardous journey. Low wages, long hours." This ad was placed in the early 1900s by the explorer Ernest Shackleton as he was looking for men to help him reach the South Pole. The ad drew more than 5,000 brave candidates.

Are you looking for a "safe" and "stable" position today? One that is secure, predictable, and nonthreatening? Maybe you're missing the best opportunities. I truly believe that if defeat or failure is not possible, then winning will not be very sweet.

A missionary society wrote to David Livingston deep in the heart of Africa and asked: "Have you found a good road to where you are? If so, we want to know how to send other men to help you." Livingston wrote back: "If you have men who will come only if they know there is a good road, I don't want them. I want men who will come if there is no road at all."

JOB SEARCH PROCESS

This phase of the process is intensive but short and focused (if you are investing 35 hours a week). And don't think that you can't complete this process while you are working. You can. Most people in a job search today are employed. Everything but the interviews themselves can be done without interfering with a normal work day. You simply need to see it as a short burst of intensive energy to lead you to the future you want.

So You Don't Have Any Experience

People are often shocked when I describe a creative job search process that may include redirecting from teaching into human resources or from practicing law to a sales and marketing position. However, we are learning more and more from employers who are disappointed when they look only at a potential employee's past experience as a predictor of future success.

Herb Greenberg, president and CEO of Caliper Corporation, a human resources consulting and psychological testing firm in Princeton, N.J., says, "From a good business perspective alone, that criteria [past experience] is an irrelevant predictor of job success."

Instead, Greenberg urges employers to consider what he calls *job matching*—evaluating the underlying strengths of job applicants, regardless of what they've been doing. In a recent study he made of 38,000 new employees in high-turnover jobs, 57 percent of those hired with experience were gone from their jobs at the end of the first year. Only 28 percent of those who were hired without experience but who were trained had left.

You can position yourself for new opportunities by highlighting areas of competence on your résumé and downplaying your job titles and history. Competencies like organizational skills, training, and customer service can position you for totally new industries and job titles.

GETTING PREPARED

Identify 30 to 40 target companies. Do you want a place with 20 to 85 employees? A profit or nonprofit organization? A manufacturing or service company? A new company or an established one? Do you want to travel or be home every evening? Would you prefer an organization in health, retail, finances, entertaining, or printing? Use the business directory for your city, the Chamber of Commerce directory, an industry guide (readily available at your local library for media, manufacturing, nonprofits, etc.) to help you create this target list. (Most libraries will have both local and national search tools for selecting companies based on your search criteria.)

You are in the driver's seat to choose the companies you would like to work with. You don't have to wait until they advertise a position or you hear someone say they are hiring. Those usual methods typically put you up against 70 to 80 people for most any desirable position, whereas in this method you may have 2 to 3 competitors. Remember: when you see an ad for a particular position, you have already lost your best opportunity for that position. Also, this is the method for finding the 87 percent of the jobs that are never advertised. In a rapidly changing workplace, everyone is looking for good people. Be proactive in your search.

Use the *three critical steps of the job search:*

1. *Send a letter of introduction to each company.* (Send no more than 15 at a time so you can do the appropriate follow-up.)

The letter of introduction is only to build name recognition. Remember, this is a selling process, and we are borrowing here from a sales technique. Let's say a company is selling water treatment systems. If they can get me to see or hear about that product at least 3 times, my likelihood of buying goes up dramatically. With the introduction letter, we are beginning the same process. You want any potential target company to see or hear about you at least 3 times. So the introduction letter is the first of at least 3 contacts in this process.

2. Send your cover letter and résumé 1 week after your introduction letter. Address the cover letter to a specific person. You can get this name from the Business Directory or call the company. Receptionists are wonderful about giving useful information if you ask nicely. Don't bother sending it to the "Personnel Department," "Human Resources," or "To Whom It May Concern." Target a person who has the ability to make a hiring decision. That will normally be the sales manager, the VP of operations, the president, the office manager, etc. Online search sites like Hoover's online (www.hoovers.com) or www.webopedia.com can give a lot of pertinent information about most companies.

3. Call to follow up. This step is very important, but only about 1 to 2 percent of job hunters do this. It is very easy to bring your name to the top of the list if you just do a follow-up call. Don't be afraid of being persistent! Call 4 to 5 days after sending your résumé. Yes, I know the challenges of screeners and voice mail. But if the process were easy, everyone would do it. You want to stand out. Don't leave messages on voice mail other than to just build in one more opportunity for repetitive name recognition. Don't say anything in this phone message about that person calling you—don't expect it and don't even set the stage for it. If you get voice mail, just hang up and call the receptionist again, saying, "I must have missed Bill. When do you expect him in today?" "What time does he normally get in the office in the morning?"

Gather any information you can. Then when you do connect in a phone call, say, "This is Bill Smith. I'm following up on a recent letter and résumé. I know what your company does and really think I could add to your success. When can we get together and talk?" You'll be surprised how frequently people will say, "Why don't you come by tomorrow at 2:00?"

Keep in mind that if you just send cover letters and résumés, you need to send out 254 to have a statistical chance of getting a job offer. If you combine that with a phone call, the number drops to 1 out of 15—a dramatic difference. Add to that an introduction letter and the results will amaze you. This is a selling process. We use a 3-time repetitive process as a marketing principle. Just commit to the process and a time line.

This process, if followed precisely, does get results. A gentleman who sent out more than 1,000 résumés over a 14-month period with no job offers was able to get 5 interviews with 3 offers in a 45-day period using this method. Another guy who had gone 6 months with no interviews received 4 offers in 10 days with this system. A recent college graduate with no real work experience received 6 job offers in a 10-day period using this process. Remember, no one is going to come looking for you. You must do an active, aggressive search. It's not uncommon for very competent professionals to resist the aggressive nature of an effective job search. They tend to assume that their credentials and great work history will speak for itself and that pushing for contacts and interviews is somehow less than professional. Unfortunately, we are in a marketing environment. It is no longer true that if you "build a better mousetrap, people will beat a path to your door." A clear plan of "selling" is required to find success in any arena. Finding a great job is no exception!

Important note: Again, don't think that I am ignoring the possibilities with the Internet. Yes, I know you can get the e-mails of 10,000 Human Resource directors and have your wonderful résumé in their mailbox this afternoon. However, I also know that 9,999 of them will resent your intrusion. And we know now that 75 percent of the companies that have hired from the Internet have had a bad experience. A professional, printed copy of your résumé in a real envelope is still the most respected method of first contact.

An irony in low unemployment times is that you may tend to think that if a company advertises a position, you are probably the only person who responded, and they will call on Monday and ask you to start work on Tuesday. That is absolutely false. Even in low unemployment, they will receive 70 to 80 responses. That tells us that although most people are working, there are still many of those same people who are in the job market. They know there are many new opportunities, so they are looking as well.

▶ Unemployed for 18 Months—What Do I Do?

If you've been unemployed for awhile, consider your self-esteem.

"People who are unemployed think the worse possible outcome is not finding another job," says Richard Bolles, author of *What Color Is Your Parachute?* (Ten Speed Press, 2003). "Actually, the worst part is losing your self-esteem. You start thinking, 'What's wrong with me?'"

Bolles says you must find ways to inject some confidence and optimism into your life because they're essential to a successful job search. He suggests a routine that includes exercise, rest, and plenty of water.

Write down 7 experiences at work that you enjoyed and list the skills that you applied in each case. According to Bolles, job hunters typically rely on only 1 or 2 methods in their search; mailing out 100 résumés or posting a copy online. Those might have worked before, but not now.

Don't limit your search to companies that have openings. Consider companies that you'd like to work for, whether they have openings or not. Contact them with the benefits you can bring.

Volunteer or shadow someone on a job you'd like. Get involved in your church and local civic clubs. "You want to take action every day, not sit around waiting for something to happen," says Bolles.

Chuck Salter, "All the Right Moves; Don't Lose Hope,"
Fast Company, July 2003 ▶

DEALING WITH JOB SEARCH DISCOURAGEMENT

You wouldn't be human if you didn't feel discouragement while you are unemployed. We attach too much of our worth and self-esteem to our jobs, and, consequently, when we are "inbetween opportunities," it's natural to feel anxious at times. But you do have daily choices: you can either convince yourself you are looking into an empty future, or you can believe that a better opportunity awaits you. I frequently tell clients that the distance between terror and exhilaration, between hope and hopelessness is often a fine line. Here are 10 tips on how to cope after a job loss:

1. Find selective places to talk honestly about your feelings.
2. Increase your knowledge about the job-search process.
3. Define what you can and cannot control.
4. Live each day fully. Take a fresh look at the success you have in areas other than work.
5. Do something for someone else. Volunteer time to worthy causes or organizations.
6. Build your own support system. Ask for help. Don't hide out in the library all day and never let your neighbors know you are looking.
7. Do something creative. Joanne and I sometimes work on big jigsaw puzzles. You'll find energy for the search if you give yourself creative breaks.
8. Maintain exercise and good nutrition.
9. Maintain hope and optimism. Set achievable daily and weekly goals. Do physical projects where you can see the results immediately.
10. Look for the larger meaning in this transition process.

Looking Around but Feeling Down

Losing a job can lead to anger, resentment, guilt, and depression. Just recently I was working with a gentleman who, having lost his job, tried to reposition himself and do a job search, only to become discouraged after just a few days with no success. He was hiding out from his wife, pretending to be doing a job search, while in reality he was going to the library to surf the Internet and read magazines. He consoled himself in fast food and high sugar snacks and quickly added about 25 pounds. This, in turn, made him self-conscious about his weight and ill-fitting clothes. "I hated my job but am still angry about being let go," he says.

This story is not unusual. New research confirms that losing a job can put people at an elevated risk for emotional and physical problems. Unemployment can start a vicious cycle of depression, loss of personal discipline, and decreased emotional health. "Depression can contribute to much longer searches," notes John Challenger, CEO of Challenger, Gray, & Christmas.

To break the cycle, take charge of the areas where you can experience immediate success. Increase physical exercise and note the satisfaction of increased vitality and creative thinking. Increase volunteering and feel the rewards of offering a helping hand. Increase positive reading and listening to inspiring audio tapes and find yourself with new ideas. Do special things for loved ones and feel their genuine support and encouragement.

None of these are directly related to getting a new job, and yet they are very much related. From these activities come the boldness, confidence, and enthusiasm necessary to present yourself well.

In this process, remember that everything prior to the interview is preliminary. No one will hire you from a résumé, nor do you want them to. Résumés and the active job search lead to interviews. Interviews get you the job.

Time spent on a good job search is time invested in your future. Don't view it casually. A week spent researching a couple of key companies so that you are more knowledgeable in the interview could mean a difference of thousands of dollars in your income in the next 2 to 3 years alone.

Learn how to do this process well; you will have to do it again. *Recognize that you must take responsibility for the success of the process.* No one can do it for you—not the government, the state, the church, or any agency. Be prepared to deal with rejection and then continue being persistent, confident that real success is just a few more contacts away.

You can find examples of the introduction letter, cover letter, and follow-up letter in the appendix.

For many of you, the Job Search Process section will be the most important piece of information in this entire book. If you understand and follow this procedure, you can dramatically transform your results, bypassing other applicants with more degrees, credentials, and experience!

▶ Dreamers, Healers, and Peacemakers

With the explosion of technology, it's easy to assume that the best jobs involve sitting at a desk using a computer. What if you don't like those jobs? Will you be lost with no opportunity? Not if you recognize new needs that are created by the technology explosion. You know how people feel when they sit at computer screens all day long? In the last 6 years the number of licensed massage therapists has quadrupled. Our schools need a major overhaul, there is crime in every community, and health care, families, and churches are full of problems that need new solutions. The solutions are not likely to be more information and more technology, but those of human touch and spiritual sensitivity.

There is an explosion of opportunities for people who are peacemakers, healers, and dreamers. Fourteen of the 30 fastest growing jobs in the next decade are for healers. The need for counseling therapists will grow dramatically as depression and major life changes confront the baby boomers as they enter the second half of their lives. Universally, people are expressing more interest in spiritual matters, giving rise for directors of religious activities and education. More than 100,000 new jobs for clergy and religious directors are expected by 2006. The demand for simpler, more humane ways of resolving disputes will expand the opportunities for dispute mediation and arbitration. As people approach middle age and have higher education levels and more disposable income, the number who go to a concert, play, or art museum at least once a year, is rising from 41 percent in 1992 to more than 51 percent today. The Bureau of Labor projects that the demand for writers, artists, and entertainers will increase 24 percent over the next decade, with a total of 772,000 new jobs in those fields.

You don't have to be a geek to succeed!

COUNTDOWN TO WORK I LOVE

1. Are some job markets more secure than others?
2. What are the best places to look for new opportunities in today's workplace?
3. What are the biggest mistakes you've made in the past in looking for new positions?
4. How do you feel about "promoting" yourself?
5. How do you know when to change jobs or careers?
6. How should we apply the principles found in Colossians 3:23–24 as workers in this day and time?

Do They Like Me?
Do I Like Them?

I learned this, at least, by my experiment: that if one advances confidently in the direction of his dreams, and endeavors to live the life which he has imagined, he will meet with a success unexpected in common hours. He will put some things behind, will pass an invisible boundary; new, universal, and more liberal laws will begin to establish themselves around and within him; or the old laws be expanded, and interpreted in his favor in a more liberal sense, and he will live with the license of a higher order of beings. . . . If you have built castles in the air, your work need not be lost; that is where they should be. Now put the foundations under them.

—HENRY DAVID THOREAU

Positions are attained through the process of an interview, yet many job seekers fail to develop good interviewing skills. Interviews are commonly viewed as a necessary evil and are approached with a great deal of anxiety and apprehension.

But change is inevitable and "security" in the workplace no longer exists, so it seems advisable to focus on developing interviewing skills to deal with these changes as smoothly as possible. Interviewing is a fine art and should be studied, prepared for, and practiced. Your ability to interview well will translate into job satisfaction and higher income.

Simply stated, a person who does not interview well will not receive a job offer. You may have an exceptional résumé and credentials and qualifications, but if you do not present yourself well in the interview, you will not receive job offers. If you cannot present yourself with confidence and project a professional image in the interview, all your preparation will have been in vain. *You must develop and practice your interviewing skills.*

Remember that in the process of a job search, you are marketing yourself. If you are uncomfortable with selling, you must prepare yourself for this process. You must have knowledge about, belief in, and enthusiasm about the product.

Contrary to popular belief, the interview is not designed to be an inquisition or interrogation. The word *interview* is derived from a Latin word that means "to see about each other." It is important to keep this definition in mind when interviewing. "To see about each other" implies that an interview is a mutual exchange of information. This exchange process not only provides the employer with the opportunity to assess your skills and qualifications, but it also provides you with the opportunity to evaluate the company and proposed position to determine if they match *your* qualifications and needs.

Do not view the interview as a one-sided process. If you are completing a well-planned job search strategy, you will have several interviews leading to 2 to 3 job offers. The interview should be an information-gathering process for you as well as the interviewer. The keys to successful interviewing are preparation, knowing what to expect, and practice. Yes, practice is a reasonable ingredient. Most of us do not interview often enough to become proficient at it. Recognizing that interviewing skills translate into satisfaction and income, you would be well advised to practice as you would at improving at golf or tennis.

PREPARATION, PREPARATION, PREPARATION

Preparation is the single most important factor in successful interviews. Your preparation should involve *2 primary components: knowing yourself and knowing the company.*

KNOWING YOURSELF

Critical to presenting yourself well and securing a position that will be meaningful and fulfilling is the process of self-assessment.

You should be intimately familiar with your (1) skills and abilities, (2) personality tendencies, and (3) values, dreams, and passions. Only by having a clear understanding of these areas will you be prepared to search in a targeted, focused direction. Obtaining a job is your goal; however, be sure that what is required in the position—and the environment connected with it—are a good fit for you, your abilities, and your interests.

Be prepared in this regard to answer the following questions in the interview (more questions will be presented later, but these few are critical in thoroughly knowing yourself):

Tell me a little about yourself. This is a standard question in almost every interview. In some ways, it is probably the most important question in your interview, and you *must* prepare your answer well in advance. The interviewer will expect you to have developed an answer for this question, and if you have not, you will appear ill-prepared, and the interview will be off to a very poor start.

This is your opportunity to sell yourself. Tell the interviewer what you want him to remember about you. You can refer to information you may want to bring up later in the interview.

An interviewer can quickly determine if you are knowledgeable and prepared or just another wandering generality hoping to land any job.

Remember, your answer to any question should be no more than *2 minutes* in length. On this particular one, you might spend 15 seconds on your personal background, 1 minute on your career highlights, a few seconds on your strongest professional achievement, and then conclude by explaining why you are looking for a new opportunity.

Ask yourself, "What can I contribute to this company?" and let that guide your response. Regardless of the content of your answer, you should outline the answer to this question on paper then practice it many times until you can repeat it concisely. Ask a friend or spouse to listen and critique it for you.

What are 3 of your strengths? If you cannot clearly identify and describe your strengths, how do you expect an interviewer to pull them out in the brief encounter of an interview?

Tell me about a weakness and what you have done to work on it. Don't play ignorant or modestly claim perfection. Be prepared to talk about something you struggle with. At the same time, stay positive in regard to what you have done to improve.

What skills do you possess that have prepared you for this job? Obviously, you need to have researched the company and the job, or you will be unprepared for this question. Again, self-assessment should have made clear identification of your skill areas and competencies.

What are your short- and long-range goals? Talk about personal goals as well as business goals. Companies today are looking for balanced individuals who are interested in things other than work. Feel free to share these goals. Talk about the opportunity to move up in the company if that is your true desire, but don't say you want to be president.

KNOWING THE COMPANY

Knowledge of the company or organization, its products and services, its standing in the community, and the key individuals involved is essential. In addition, you should obtain information about the company's annual growth rate, annual sales, number of employees, location of the company headquarters, and its major changes such as buyouts or mergers and industry trends. The information you have, which will lead to questions you can ask, can easily tip the scales in your favor during the interview.

The following sources will help you in locating company information:

- annual reports—available for the asking from any major company
- business periodicals (*Wall Street Journal, Forbes, Fortune,* etc.)
- industry magazines
- *Dun's Regional Business Directory* magazine
- City business directory (available in any major city; lists size, year started, number of employees, contact principals)

- Hoover's Business Directory (get all the business directory information and more; latest stock quotes, quarterly earnings, SEC filings, compensation figures, etc.) at www.hoovers.com
- Moody's Manuals
- Standard & Poor's publications, including *Standard & Poor's Register of Directors & Executives*
- *Thomas Register of manufacturers annual reports* (see www.thomasregister.com)
- Better Business Bureau reports
- Chamber of Commerce publications
- Current employees (valuable source for obtaining information)
- Bank of America Small Business Resource Centers (a wonderful resource for in-depth information about any company or organization in the United States)

Most of these reference materials can be found in any major library or on the Internet.

Interviewing Flubs

I am continually amazed at what people actually do in interview situations.

OfficeTeam (www.officeteam.com), a worldwide staffing company, recently hired an independent research firm to survey hiring executives at the 1,000 largest U.S. companies. The question: What are the strangest things that job candidates have said or done in interviews? Here are some of their more memorable answers:

- After answering the first few questions, the candidate picked up his cell phone and called his parents to let them know the interview was going well.
- The person got up just a few minutes after the interview had begun, saying he left his dog in the car and needed to check on him.
- When asked why she wanted to work for the company, the candidate replied, "That's a good question. I really haven't given it much thought."

- When asked how he would improve sales if hired, the candidate replied, "I'll have to think about that and get back to you." He then stood up, walked out, and never came back.
- Asked by the hiring manager why he was leaving his current job, the candidate replied, "My manager is a jerk. All managers are jerks."
- When the interviewer asked what the candidate was earning, she answered, "I really don't see how that is any of your business."
- After being complimented on his choice of college and the GPA he achieved, the candidate replied, "I'm glad that got your attention. I didn't really go there."
- The candidate asked for an early morning interview. He showed up with a box of doughnuts and ate them during the interview, saying this was the only time he'd have to eat breakfast before going to work.
- When asked by the hiring manager about his career goals, the candidate replied, "To work the least amount of time possible until I can get your job."

Need I say that none of these folks were hired? The moral, according to OfficeTeam executive director Liz Hughes: "Think before you speak. The first thing that comes to your mind might not be the most appropriate thing to share with the hiring manager." How true.

INTERVIEW INTRICACIES

FIRST IMPRESSIONS

Ten seconds after you've walked into the room, before you even get a chance to sit down, you may have won or lost the job. While you may courteously be given an hour to answer questions and describe your accomplishments, studies indicate the interviewer forms a strong positive or negative impression of you within seconds of greeting you. One university study had job interviewers indicate when they had made a decision by pushing a button on a timer. *Every interviewer pushed the timer within 10 seconds.* This lets us know it's not the fine print on the fourth page of your résumé but other factors that take precedence in making the hiring decision.

After that first decision, interviewers tend to gather information to support the decision they have already made. In these first few minutes of an interview, the employer is asking, "Do I like this person? Do I trust this person? Is this person fun to be around?" Although it may be camouflaged, this is where the focus lies more than "Does this person have an MBA in marketing?"

Here are some suggestions to help you create a positive impression:

- The interviewer will schedule the time for the interview and the place where it will be conducted. If you are allowed to choose the time, avoid Monday mornings and Friday afternoons. Choose morning appointments. Research shows that 83 percent of executives are more likely to hire A.M. job seekers. And 70 percent of all hiring decisions are made before 11:00 A.M. So obviously, if you can suggest the time of an interview, make it before 11:00 A.M. Afternoon appointments should be set no later than 1 hour prior to the close of the normal business day. Again, on Monday, people tend to have too much to do and on Friday they are anticipating the weekend and ready to get out of the office. So the best times for interviews are Tuesday, Wednesday, or Thursday mornings between 8:00 and 10:00.
- Know the exact time and location of the interview.
- Be punctual; arrive 5 to 15 minutes early. Don't go in too early, but arrive early enough so you have the opportunity to observe the environment and determine if you would enjoy working there. (Interviewers will be annoyed as much by your arriving very early as by arriving late. Do neither.) To arrive too early indicates overanxiousness; to arrive late is inconsiderate. The only sensible solution is to arrive at the interview on time but at the location early. That allows you time to visit the rest room and make any

necessary adjustments to your comfort and appearance. Take a couple of minutes to relax and prepare mentally.

- Know the name and title of the interviewer. Do not use first names unless asked.

The 5 Fatal Flaws in Interviewing

Don't assume the interview is only a formality. In fact, it's the beginning of the selling process. Your résumé has gotten you an interview; now you have a chance to actually make them want you for a position. Be careful of committing the following flaws.

Lack of enthusiasm: You don't have to be a Zig Ziglar or a David Letterman, but you must express enthusiasm for a job if you don't want to be weeded out immediately. Enthusiasm, boldness, and confidence will often do more for you in an interview than another college degree.

What's in it for me? We know you want to know about benefits, vacations, etc., but don't lead with these questions. First, the employer will want to know what you can do for them. You can't negotiate for more vacation time before you have been offered a job. Convince the employer that you are the right person for the job, be sure that you want to work there, then you can discuss pay and benefits.

Unclear job goals: Don't be a generalist. Be clear about the job you are seeking. If the interviewer gets the impression that you are just looking for a job rather than a specific opportunity to use your skills, you will sabotage your chances. You should be able to state without hesitation 3 characteristics that would make you a great candidate for any given job you are applying for.

Poor personal appearance: The key here is to fit in with the organization you are contacting. I will defend your right to wear cutoffs and a baseball cap, but if you really want a job, you must dress appropriately. Many times I hear people who are irritated about not being given a job when they have a nose ring, bad breath, and unshined shoes. Keep in mind that organizations hire people, not credentials and experience. If they don't like you, it

doesn't matter how great your experience is, you won't get the
job.

Not selling yourself: Even if you would not enjoy selling vacuum cleaners door-to-door, you have to realize that in the interview process, you are selling yourself. Especially in today's market, you have to promote yourself. Follow up immediately with a
thank-you note and a telephone call 3 or 4 days later. It's a good
way to reinforce your interest in the job as well as ask a question
or 2 you may have forgotten in the interview.

DRESS, ETIQUETTE, AND BODY LANGUAGE

We have already established that an interviewer decides within
the first few minutes if he likes you. While some of the reasons
may be subtle and intangible, we can control some of the more
obvious ones to your advantage. The impression you want to create for the interviewer is directly reflected in the way you dress
and in the way you handle yourself. Therefore, appropriate dress,
mannerisms, and behavior are important variables.

Appropriate Dress

There is only one way to dress for the first meeting: clean cut
and conservative. You may not see yourself that way, and you
know your right to look otherwise, but this is not the time to make
a statement about your rights. I am still amazed at the number of
people who sabotage any chance of being hired simply by not
making the effort to make a good first impression. *Your task is to
understand how others see you.*

- Have your hair trimmed neatly.
- Shower or bathe as close to the interview time as possible.
  Use deodorant but not aftershave or perfume. You are try-
  ing to get hired not courted.
- Be conservative on jewelry. Do not appear ostentatious or
  flamboyant.
- Make sure shoes are neat and shined. Avoid worn belts,
  frayed collars, and ragged pockets.

- Use a small breath mint if you have a bad taste in your mouth. If you smoke, by all means, use a mint. Be aware that cigarette smoke permeates your clothing and hair. A strong odor may be offensive to a prospective employer.

Etiquette

Try to make the interview as comfortable as possible. Sit straight in the chair, be relaxed, and do not fidget. Use a firm, moderate tone when speaking. Make direct eye contact with the interviewer. Few things will sabotage your efforts quicker than poor eye contact. This is always perceived as shifty and dishonest. Obviously, avoid profanity or off-color comments. Avoid slang or cultural colloquialisms ("fixin', I done this, ain't nobody"). These may appear cute on TV but are seen as very unprofessional in the real world.

Body Language

Think "up." Prior to the interview, focus on being "up" and on having your body language reflect being "up." Keep your head up, your shoulders up, and your body straight. This posture sends a positive message, conveying energy and enthusiasm. Match your energy with that of the person interviewing you. It's OK to be confident and to speak up. You can have energetic body language. Don't come across as condescending or intimidating, but do be confident.

Smiling for Dummies

An old Chinese saying goes something like this: "A man without a smiling face must not open a shop." I recently ate lunch at a brand new restaurant in Franklin, Tennessee. No one smiled or greeted me when I came in or during my entire stay there. However, there is another established restaurant with the same menu format where I am greeted with enthusiasm every time I visit. Guess where I will go next time.

That same phenomenon has a similar effect on interviewers. In a survey of 5,000 human resource managers, one of the questions was, What do you look for most in a candidate? Of the 2,756 who responded, 2,322 ranked enthusiasm first. The first thing interviewers look for in a candidate is vitality and enthusiasm. Many candidates with the right background experience and skills disqualify themselves with a demeanor that suggests they lack energy.

The easiest way to convey energy and enthusiasm is to smile. Now there's a tip that you can implement today. No waiting, no paying for expensive degrees, no buying a new suit—just smile.

In the classic little book *The Magic of Thinking Big,* David Schwartz challenges readers with this test: "Try to feel defeated and smile big at the same time. You can't. A big smile gives you confidence. A big smile beats fear, rolls away worry, defeats despondency." That sounds like a great preparation for your next interview.

Body language is 55 percent of the communication process. Communication can be enhanced or hindered by standing too close or too far away or being too animated or frigid.

Practice your handshake. A weak handshake indicates a weak personality. Reach for full palm-to-palm contact. Don't offer only fingers or grab only fingers.

Sit comfortably in the chair. Don't get too relaxed and slouch down. Sit straight and lean forward slightly. This shows interest and energy. When you are excited about something you are relating, lean forward in your chair. When you want to show that you are very knowledgeable and confident, then you should lean back, and that will indicate your expertise. Sit with your arms comfortably in your lap or on the chair arms. Do not cross your arms; this is still universally seen as closing off or holding back.

Do not put your hands to your mouth. This is perceived as a deceptive gesture, showing that you're trying to hide the truth. Avoid repetitive gestures. Avoid pointing or any excessive movements.

Tone of voice is 38 percent of the communication process. Excessive tone ranges, loudness, or softness can open or close the doorway of communication.

Be aware of unique personal habits. (I recently interviewed a client who had a very annoying, sucking-sound laugh, which she offered approximately every 30 seconds. She was totally taken aback when I mentioned it and was genuinely unaware of its effect.)

Words make up only 7 percent of the communication process. The proper words can effectively communicate your message but only with proper body language and tone of voice.

Do not be uncomfortable with silence. Experienced interviewers may purposely allow silence to see how you respond. Use the silence to rehearse what you may want to offer or what you may want to ask.

Watch the overuse of "uh-huh" or filler words. I once coached a struggling salesman who seemed to think that controlling the conversation was an effective selling technique. Without drawing attention to it, I counted his saying "basically" 19 times in a 3-minute period. He had allowed this 1 word to be used as a quick filler anytime his mind was momentarily blank. Trust me; silence is better than the obnoxious overuse of a filler word.

THE INTERVIEW PROCESS

Six general rules will help you in this process.

Smile. Few things convey pleasantness, enthusiasm, and comfort like a smile. Successful people smile a lot. People who frown are not perceived as happy, productive professionals.

Be pleasant and outgoing. Do not attempt to take over the interview but respond easily and spontaneously to questions.

Show self-confidence. Fidgeting, nervousness, glancing down, not accepting compliments, and self-deprecating statements all convey poor self-confidence.

Do not run down former employers or coworkers. Prepare positive reasons for leaving any former position.

Show sincere interest in the company and the interviewer. Remember, your task is to sell yourself to the interviewer, not to just convince them you are the best candidate for the position.

Know your résumé thoroughly. Be prepared to elaborate on part of it. Keep in mind that you are selling yourself in the interview process. Effective salespeople know their product, conduct research to determine their customer's needs, and use that knowledge to sell their product. During the interview, the employer or company is the customer and you take on the role of the salesperson. Just as products do not sell themselves, neither do job candidates.

Note: Much of this may sound like a very old-fashioned approach to interviewing—conservative dress, watching posture, not chewing gum, etc. And it is! We are seeing a return to the embracing of these and other "traditional" values. Many companies are discontinuing "casual days" and are encouraging a more professional look. The casualness of recent years has backfired in lowering customer confidence. So in the interviewing process you can tip the scale in your favor by leaning toward the conservative side.

THE WARM-UP

The interviewer may initiate some small talk about non-controversial matters. Many times the interviewer will find something on your résumé to talk about. Warm-up topics may include weather, sports, or one of your hobbies. The purpose of this warm-up is to help you feel relaxed and to develop a comfortable atmosphere, so you will speak freely and spontaneously about yourself. Remember, however, that from the first instant, you are being evaluated, even if you are not covering issues pertinent to the position.

QUESTION AND ANSWER

The question-and-answer section usually takes up approximately 75 percent of the interview process. The candidate is asked to review her qualifications as presented on the résumé. (Remember that anything presented on the résumé is fair game, so be ready to discuss it. Thus, it's important to have on your résumé *only* items that are sales tools for where you want to go.) After questions about your qualifications and skills, the interviewer will provide you with information about the company. Ideally, you then will be given an opportunity to ask questions. By all means, have 4 to 5 questions ready to ask. The questions you ask may create more of an impression than how you answered the previous ones.

Questions Asked by the Interviewer

The following are some sample interview questions. Write out your answers to these questions; just thinking about them is not sufficient preparation for the actual answering. Writing your answers will help you be more comfortable handling the same or similar questions in the interview. Remember, the interview is not just a formality since the interviewer has seen your great résumé; *the interview is the most important part of the whole process.* Prepare a 1- to 2-minute response to each question. If you take longer than that, the interviewer may feel you are taking control of the interview.

1. Tell me a little about yourself.
2. What are your greatest strengths? What are 3 characteristics that would make you a good candidate for this position?
3. What would your previous employer list as your greatest strengths?
4. What motivates you to put forth your greatest effort?
5. What have been some of your most significant accomplishments? How were you able to achieve those accomplishments?
6. What have you done that has contributed to increased sales, profits, efficiency, etc.?
7. What types of situations frustrate you? What are your weaknesses? What have you attempted and failed to accomplish?
8. What are you looking for in a new position? Why do you want this job? What do you find attractive about this position?
9. Why are you leaving your current job?
10. What important changes or trends do you see in this industry? How do you think those changes will affect the way we succeed in this company?

11. How long would it take you to make a meaningful contribution to our company? What are the areas in which you would need more training? Do you feel you may be overqualified or too experienced for this position?

12. What do you look for in a supervisor? Describe the relationship that should exist between a supervisor and his employee. What do you see as your most difficult task as a manager? What is your management style?

13. Do you prefer working alone or as part of a team? Are you better working with things, people, or ideas? Are you better at creating or doing?

14. Describe an ideal working environment. In your last position, what were the things you liked most/least? How do you handle pressure and deadlines?

15. Where, on your list of priorities, does your job fall? What kind of things outside of work do you enjoy? What magazines do you like to read? Name 3 books you have read in the last year. Are you achieving personal goals you have set?

16. Where would you like to be 5 years from now? What would you expect to be earning 5 years from now? Are you continuing your education? How are you staying current with changes in this industry?

17. How long do you feel a person should stay in the same position?

18. What does a typical weekend consist of for you? What do you do to relieve boredom?

19. What other kinds of positions have you been looking at? If we do not select you for this position, would you be interested in another (office, sales, administrative, etc.) position with this company? How does this job compare with others for which you have interviewed? What makes this job different from your current/last one?

20. Why should we choose you for this position? What can you do for us that someone else cannot do?

21. Do you have any questions? (A good interviewer will ask you this.)

Make sure you are ready with 4 to 5 questions. Even if the interviewer has answered everything you need to know, it will make you appear more interested and more knowledgeable if you ask a few questions.

Have You Always Been This Fat?

A London travel agent wanted to set up a coffee bar for his staff. He wrote a help wanted ad that read: "We require a friendly person with a flair for preparing fresh sandwiches and making soups for a team that deserves simple but special lunches."

The local job center refused to run the ad as written. The travel agency owner was informed that he couldn't advertise for a "friendly" catering manager because "that would discriminate against applicants not lucky enough to have that sort of personality."

We know that 85 percent of a person's success in the workplace is due to personal skills and only 15 percent is due to technical skills. Interviewers do look at personal traits, even if they resist asking some of the questions they'd like to. Here are some tricky ones that may surprise you.

When was the last time you used illegal drugs? An employer may ask applicants about current and prior illegal use of drugs. An individual who is currently using illegal drugs is not protected under the American Disabilities Act. For example, an employer may ask an applicant: "Do you currently use illegal drugs? Have you ever used illegal drugs? What illegal drugs have you used in the last 6 months?"

How old are you? This is an illegal question. However, it is lawful to ask, "What year did you graduate from high school?" A little simple math ought to provide any desired information regarding the age issue.

What are your family plans? is another illegal question. But you can ask, "Where do you see yourself 5 years from now?"

What church do you go to? What religion are you? No job-related considerations justify asking about religious beliefs or convictions unless your organization is a religious institution, in which case you may give preference to individuals of your own religion.

What is your height? What is your weight? The EEOC and the courts have ruled minimum height and weight requirements to be illegal if they screen out a disproportionate number of minority group individuals or women, and the employer cannot show that these standards are essential to the safe performance of a job in question.

The Only 5 Interviewing Questions That Matter

In *What Color Is Your Parachute?* Richard Bolles says there are really only 5 critical questions that employers are dying to know:

1. Why are you here?
2. What can you do for us?
3. What kind of person are you?
4. What distinguishes you from 19 other people who can do the same tasks that you can?
5. Can I afford you?

Unusual Interview Questions

As companies return to interviewing processes that help them understand the whole person, some questions being asked may appear to be a little unusual. The questions may be designed to discover what you value, how you think, or just to see how you respond to a question without a clear answer.

1. What's the biggest career mistake you've made so far?
2. Who else are you interviewing with, and how close are you to accepting an offer?
3. What's the last book you've read?
4. Why do they make manhole covers round?
5. If I stood you next to a skyscraper and gave you a barometer, how could you figure out how tall the building was?
6. If you had your own company, what would it do?

7. You have 2 containers; 1 holds 5 gallons, the other 3. You can have as much water as you want. Your task is to measure exactly 4 gallons of water into the 5-gallon container.

8. You wake up 1 morning and there's been a power outage. You know you have 12 black socks and 8 blue ones. How many socks do you need to pull out before you've got a match?

9. How many barbers are there in Chicago?

10. How many cubes are at the center of a Rubik's Cube?

Keep in mind any company is interested in hiring the whole person, not just your technical, administrative, computer, or sales skills.

Questions to Ask the Interviewer

In today's marketplace, it is not enough to competently answer the interviewer's questions. You would be well advised to have prepared 4 to 5 questions to ask when given the opportunity. *People who ask questions appear brighter, more interested, and more knowledgeable.*

1. What would be a typical day's assignments?

2. What are the travel requirements, if any?

3. What is the typical career path in this position? What is a realistic timeframe for advancement?

4. Where are the opportunities for greatest growth within the company?

5. What criteria are used to evaluate and promote employees here?

6. What type of training is available?

7. What kind of ongoing professional development programs are available to help me continue to grow?

8. Whom would I report to in this position? What can you tell me about that person's management style?

9. What management philosophy is used by the company?

10. How would you describe the company's culture (personality, environment)?

11. What is the company's mission statement? What are the company's goals?
12. What are the skills and attributes most needed to advance in this company?
13. Who will be this company's major competitors over the next 5 years? How will this company maintain an advantage over them?
14. What has been the growth pattern of this company over the last 5 years?
15. What do you see as upcoming changes in this industry?
16. Is this a new position, or would I be replacing someone?
17. What qualities are you looking for in the right person for this position?
18. Is there a written job description? May I see it?
19. How many people are in this department?
20. How do you see me complementing the existing group?
21. What do you enjoy about working for this company?

Louder Than Words

We are seeing an increasing creativity in interviewing today. Many interviewers have a favorite question: "Why are manhole covers round? How many barbers are there in Chicago? If you could be an animal, what would it be?" Some interviewers are big on nonverbal clues. J. C. Penney was famous for taking potential hires out to breakfast. If the interviewee put salt and pepper on his food before tasting it, the interview was over. Mr. Penney believed that such actions revealed a person who made decisions before he had all the evidence.

Jeff O'Dell of August Technology often asks candidates out to lunch and suggests that they drive. "How organized someone's car is is an amazing indicator of how organized the rest of their life is," he says. O'Dell believes that the best job candidates not only will have clean cars—"no Slim-Fast cans or tennis balls rolling around in the backseat"—but will also excel at casual conversation in a restaurant. "It's a way to learn the personal side of things—whether they have a family, [whether] they smoke, etc." that doesn't come out in the formal interview.

Dave Hall doesn't mind making candidates a little more nervous than they already are. Hall, a principal at Search Connection, likes to place want ads that list his company's name but not its phone number; he wants only candidates who'll bother to look the number up. When he's not entirely sure about candidates after their interviews, he instructs them to call him to follow up—and then doesn't return their first 3 calls. He says he's looking for employees who'll persist through a million no-thank-yous in making recruiting calls.

Exiting the Interview

As you prepare to leave, stand up straight and tall, shake hands, and then pick up your notebook. Make sure the exiting handshake is strong. Practice what you are going to say. Don't be afraid to ask what the next step will be. Have a closing well rehearsed. Ask, "What will be the next step? When can I expect a decision to be made? May I call you on Thursday?" Keep your body oriented toward the interviewer even as you are leaving. Continue to make eye contact until you turn to exit. Do not ask about salary and benefits at this time. Summarize your qualifications. Also, state whether you do or do not still want the job. Use this wrap-up as a time to show the interviewer that you have listened and heard what has been said about the company and the position. Make a closing statement that ties in all the information you have obtained from the interview.

Very few people receive offers after a first interview. Therefore, it is very important that you initiate your own follow-up with the interviewer. Your persistence and initiative may be the one small difference in making you the candidate of choice.

Nine out of 10 candidates still do not follow up on their interviews. The follow-up letter provides you with a great opportunity to once again put your name at the top of the candidate pool. The thank-you or follow-up letter is to express appreciation for the time of the interviewer and to confirm your interest in the position. It will also help the interviewer remember you clearly and demonstrate your professionalism and writing skills. Remember that with the introduction letter, cover letter and résumé, phone follow-up, interview, and now the follow-up letter, you have created 5 contact points with the person making the decision. Your name will be hard to forget.

Mention in the letter that you will keep in touch and indicate on what day you will make your first call. For example, "I will check back with you on Tuesday, August 23, to see if you require any additional information." Mail the follow-up letter no later than the next day following the interview.

Continue to make follow-up contacts every 4 to 5 days following an interview until a decision has been made. Having invested your time in the interview, you have earned the right to know what decisions have been made. Decisions are frequently made slowly in any organization. Don't be too quick to assume you are not being considered. Your persistent follow-up may ultimately make you the candidate of choice.

COUNTDOWN TO WORK I LOVE

1. Can you clearly and easily describe your strongest areas of competence?
2. Does knowing that interviewing means "to see about each other" make it more comfortable to ask for information about the company and the position?
3. Are you aware of any personal habits or annoying filler words that may be part of your personal presentation?
4. Is your level of enthusiasm contagious?
5. What are some unusual questions you know of that have been asked of you or others in an interviewing situation? (You only have to pull out 3 socks to be guaranteed a match. And there's really no accurate way to know how many barbers there are in Chicago. It's just one of those questions designed to see how you approach a difficult task.)

6. How can you be humble and godly and still show confidence?
7. Would you ever take a position even if you knew it was not a good fit for you?

Show Me the Money

I can do something
I am but one,
But I am one,
I cannot do everything,
But I can do something.
What I can do
I ought to do.
And what I ought to do,
With God's help,
I will do.

—ANONYMOUS

I have learned that success is to be measured not so much by the
position that one has reached in life as by the obstacles which he has
overcome while trying to succeed.

—BOOKER T. WASHINGTON

The phrase "show me the money" was widely popularized by the movie *Jerry Maguire.* In the movie, Cuba Gooding Jr. plays a professional football player and Tom Cruise is his agent. No matter what great position Tom would negotiate for Cuba, the bottom line was Cuba shouting, *"Show me the money!"* It was a funny and memorable line in the movie, but how do we approach it in our own work life?

Is it always self-serving, egotistical, and materialistic to say, "Show me the money"? Or is it a part of the process that we can learn to do well and in a way that is win-win for everyone involved? Why is it that people with the same title of "administrative assistant" earn anywhere from $18,000 to $80,000 per year. Some attorneys charge $40 per hour and some $400 per hour. Is there really that much difference in ability or training? What is reasonable to expect for the work you do?

How much initiative can you take in this process? Are salaries, bonuses, hourly wages, and benefits written in stone in every com-

> *"A wise man should have money in his head, but not in his heart."*
> — *Jonathan Swift*

pany? The answer to that last question is a resounding *no*. Compensation is a very fluid concept and one that can be negotiated in nearly every situation. Finding the right compensation package is still part of the interviewing process.

The first issue to be recognized is that you must totally believe that you are the best person for the position. That comes from being clear on your areas of competence and from having the confidence, enthusiasm, and boldness that can come only from having a clear focus. Then you are ready to present yourself in the most advantageous way. There can be nothing phony in how you see yourself fitting into the position in question. You cannot be enthusiastic about a position you don't believe is a good match for you. And you can't be confident about doing something you don't really believe in. The biggest stumbling block for people in negotiating a reasonable compensation is that they don't really want the position or don't really believe they are the absolute best person for the job. In previous chapters we discussed how important it is to make a proper match between the work and what you offer. And yes, now it's time to focus on *the work you love.*

Here's the convoluted thinking of how we often approach work: *Work is work. I have to just find a job to pay the bills. If I really did what I love doing, my family would live on beans and rice.*

Isn't that the typical belief? But guess what? It's not true. Those who move toward the work they love tend to find not only a sense of fulfillment, meaning, and accomplishment, but often find a dam break in terms of what happens financially. Should it be easier to make money doing something you love or something you hate?

In Dr. Thomas Stanley's wonderful book *The Millionaire Mind,* he relates how this issue is lived out by those who are now decamillionaires. Most love their chosen vocations, or, as one of the wealthier members stated, "It is not work; it is a labor of love." Imagine that.

Dr. Stanley also says it's hard for a person to recognize opportunities if he stays in one place and remains in one job—most self-made millionaires have had a rather wide experience with various part-time and temporary jobs. And finally, if you are creative enough to select the ideal vocation, you win big time. The really brilliant millionaires are those who selected a vocation that they love—one that has few competitors but generates high profits. *If you love, absolutely love, what you are doing, chances are excellent that you will succeed.*

> *"I have enough money to last me the rest of my life, unless I buy something."*
> — *Jackie Mason*

So you've endured the job search process, and now a company wants to have you on board. With the interviewing process coming to an end, it's time to deal with the burning question of compensation. You are thinking, *How much can I get here?* and the employer is thinking, *How much is this person going to cost me?*

Don't discuss salary until

- you know exactly what the job requires,
- they have decided they want you, and
- you have decided you want them.

The responsibilities of the job determine the salary, not

- your education,
- your experience, or
- your previous salary.

To win at the salary negotiation, don't be the first one to bring it up. Instead:

- Show genuine interest in what the job requires.
- Refrain from asking about benefits, vacations, perks, etc., until you know you want the job.
- Say, "Let's talk a little more about the position to see if there's a match," if they ask too early what you need.

Recognize that many things can fall under the title of compensation:

- a company car (preferably a BMW)
- a country club or YMCA membership
- free life insurance
- a medical plan
- a dental and vision plan
- profit sharing
- company stock
- an expense account
- tuition reimbursement
- additional time off
- relocation expenses
- your own laptop computer
- your own administrative assistant
- a free parking space
- a sign-on bonus
- weekly massages
- 2 weeks in the company condo in Hawaii
- a Rolex watch after 90 days
- your birthday off
- a production bonus upon completion of a project
- educational opportunities for your children
- a cell phone for business and personal use
- 401(k) contributions
- a low-interest loan for home purchase

You get the idea. Make this a fun process. I realize that negotiating anything is not very comfortable for some of you. If you don't enjoy going to Tijuana and bargaining for the turquoise necklace you want, you may be somewhat intimidated by this process. But realize that negotiating salary is not a confrontational process and certainly not a win/lose proposition.

Company Perks—A Brand New BMW?

Believe it or not, in today's desperate scramble for good employees, a BMW is not impossible. In fact, it's a reality at

Revenue Systems Inc. in Alpharetta, Georgia. All 45 employees—
from secretaries to managers—get to drive a brand-new leased
BMW at the company's expense. The company simply knew what
their average recruiting costs were and put the money into the
luxury car leases instead. The response from applicants—thousands of whom have sent in their résumés—would be enough to
make other CEOs green with envy.

Ceil Diaz left her job working for the state of Illinois to join a
Chicago ad firm. There she receives a basket of flowers and gift
certificates on her 1-year job anniversary and got to meet with
architects to help plan her work space. John Nuveen & Co., a
Chicago investment bank, pays the bulk of college tuition for the
children of employees who have been with the company for at
least 5 years. How would you like to have someone walk your
dog? What about an errand runner to pick up groceries for your
family? Built in day care and on-site $3.00 haircuts?

Starting to make that annual Thanksgiving turkey look a little
slim, huh?

Try this scenario. Let's say Bob goes out to buy a car. He looks
at a Toyota Camry and decides that is what he wants. It's a basic
model with no extras but seems to be a good buy on a dependable
car to get him back and forth to school. Once he decides on the
car, there are two possibilities:

The first is an inexperienced salesperson will breathe a sigh of
relief and lead Bob into the finance and insurance office before he
changes his mind. He will take his little commission and go on to
the next buyer.

In the second possibility, a mature, experienced salesperson
will talk with Bob, asking if he has a favorite kind of music. Of
course Bob does. "Wouldn't it be nice to have a great sound system in this car?" the salesman asks. "With spring just around the
corner, you know how much you would enjoy a sunroof. Since
you are in school, it will be very important to make this car last
for a long time. It would be advisable to have fabric protection,
undercoating, and rust-proofing applied. For those long trips

back home to family, wouldn't it be nice to have cruise control?" And so on. Ultimately, Bob walks out, a happy customer, but with a purchase price of $1,500 more than he had originally agreed to. Has he been tricked? Of course not. He has simply been shown the benefits of some things he really did want. In the same way, once the company has made its initial decision to hire you, you can freely discuss additional benefits and compensation with little fear of changing the company's basic decision that it wants you!

I recently worked with a young lady who had lost her job, in which she earned over $70,000. Panicked and convinced she could never find another job in that income range, she had decided she would have to start her own business. However, after identifying her unique areas of competence, I advised against that and encouraged her to do a creative job search. In a short period of time she had 2 offers on the table; the clearly better fit offered her a base salary of $89,000. We discussed the offer, the fact that it was a great fit, and she went back and asked for $98,000. They settled at a base of $94,000 with some additional benefits, bringing her package to approximately $105,000.

What are you doing in the salary-negotiating process? Keep in mind that if you have handled the interview as described, salary did not come up until you decided you wanted the job and the hiring manager decided he wanted you. At that point, and not until that point, you are in a position to negotiate. Also, keep in mind that if you have done an effective job search, you should be talking with more than 1 company anyway. Here is the timing for discussing salary. Speak at the peak.

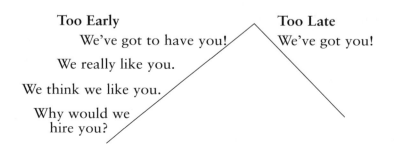

Too Early　　　　　　　　　　　**Too Late**
We've got to have you!　　　We've got you!
We really like you.
We think we like you.
Why would we
hire you?

Poverty Living or Excellence?

The Economic Policy Institute (www.epinet.org) recently identified what they call a "living wage." They say $30,000 is needed
for a family of 4. This accounts for a telephone, health insurance,
and child care, but does not include restaurant meals, video
rentals, Internet access, or vacations. That means someone has
to be making $14 an hour or more than one person in the home
has to be working. It may come as a surprise to know that 60
percent of American workers do not make $14 an hour.
Incidentally, the government shows $18,400 as the official 2003
poverty level for a family of 4. The troubling range is between
$18,400 and $30,000 where a family is not eligible for government assistance but clearly has difficulty making ends meet.

So the resulting questions are, How can I have areas of competence worth $14 per hour? Who else in the home is going to
work? How can I add to my income? How can I escape the
hourly income trap?

Fortunately, there are opportunities in all these questions. You
may not choose to have a second person in the home in a traditional job. Do you have areas of competence that you are over-
looking? I once worked with a lady with a high school education
in an $8-per-hour job. We looked for unique areas of expertise.
She realized she was proficient in both Spanish and English and
now books herself an average of 20 hours weekly at $50 per
hour as a medical environment interpreter. If you clean houses
for a cleaning service, you will likely be paid $7 to $9 per hour.
But most of those cleaning services bill their clients at $25 to $35
per hour. If you can find 4 or 5 clients yourself, you may be able
to cut your hours in half and double your income. Are you familiar
with how Internet auctions work? I recently worked with a guy
who had purchased a book for $6 and sold it on eBay for $150 to
add to his meager income.

Don't get trapped or feel like a victim. You may never get
ahead in an hourly job. Roughly 70 percent of jobs held by people
with less than a high school diploma experienced negative real

wage growth in the last 2 years; even with college graduates, 56 percent are in jobs with no real wage growth likely.

For more information, check all the free articles at www.48days.ibelieve.com.

At this point, you should be prepared. You should know what comparable salaries are for the position you are considering. (Check Internet salary sites listed in the appendix.) That and the responsibilities of the position determine what your compensation should be. A couple of years ago, I worked with a young lady who had been fired from a position in which she made $19,000 per year for clerical work. She decided that wasn't what she wanted to do anyway and began to get focused on what she did want. It was somewhat of a redirection, but she was enthusiastic and confident. After having done an excellent job search, she began interviewing for positions in graphic design and marketing. She interviewed for a position advertised at $32,500. She came out of that interview with a salary package of $54,000. The company does not know to this day that in her last job she was making $19,000, nor does it need to know. That has nothing to do with what she is being paid now. She relayed the benefits of what she had to offer and was compensated based on the value of that.

> *"I'm living so far beyond my income that we may almost be said to be living apart."*
> — e. e. cummings

Always focus on the job you are going to, not where you are coming from. There is no law that says your pay will increase by only 4 percent a year or even 10 percent. The world is a very giving place, and if you can convey your benefits, the world will give you what you are worth. Many of my clients have increased their compensation dramatically because they learned to focus on what they were going to rather than looking at what they came from.

Also, recognize that your *needs* are *not* the determinant of how you are paid. If you apply at Taco Bell, it is irrelevant whether you have a $1,200 per month house payment and a $450 per month car note; Taco Bell is not going to pay you $40,000 per year. Your needs are not the company's concern. Recently a young lady come into my office in distress. She had spoken to her boss that morning, explaining that she had just moved into a nicer apartment and purchased a new car and could no longer manage on what they were paying her. They fired her on the spot. And I laughed when she told me this story. I totally agreed with the company. What she did to obligate herself to higher payments had nothing to do with how she should be paid.

Be sure you know your value and then market yourself in that range. In my experience, I find that people often give themselves about a $10,000 window from which to work. If they have been making $30,000, they will look at positions that pay about $25,000 to $35,000. But if they see a perfectly matched position paying $65,000, they don't bother to apply. Be careful of setting your own limitations. You will end up pretty much where you expect to end up.

Getting Paid What You're Worth

How do you describe what you're worth? Is it based on your age, 4 times your mortgage payment, your degrees, your years of experience, or your past salary history? None of these matter. The only criteria for determining your value today is your current contribution and level of responsibility.

I've coached lots of people into significantly higher levels of compensation by using the phrase, "Based on the level of responsibility you describe, I would see that in the —— to —— range. Is that still within your budget?"

The biggest mistake people make in negotiating salary is to discuss it too soon. Do whatever you can to avoid talking about salary until you get the job offer. Anything prior to that will work against you.

Also, the best to-the-point book on this I have ever found is *Negotiating Your Salary: How to Make $1,000 a Minute* by Jack Chapman. Order it on our site at www.48days.com/products.php. And see the appendix for Web sites on salary.

Keep these principles in mind:

1. You must make the company money. As a rule of thumb, you must make the company 3 to 5 times your salary for your hiring to be worthwhile.

2. Your compensation almost always relates to your level of responsibility. If it's easy to replace you, you aren't worth a whole lot.

3. Your work is an intangible. Few salaries are written in concrete. Companies that budget $38,000 for a position will start out trying to hire someone for $31,000. Recognize that the first offer is probably not what the company has in the budget.

4. Once you agree on a package, get it in writing. If you have been creative in this process, it is necessary to write out what you verbally agreed on. That way, you don't have to defend later what you thought was said.

Have fun in the process. Don't say yes until everything matches your goals. If you've done a great job search, you should be considering 2 to 3 offers.

COUNTDOWN TO WORK I LOVE

1. Is negotiating on price uncomfortable for you? Describe 3 things for which you negotiated the purchase price.

2. Have you negotiated your income in the past?

3. Do you realize that in changing companies you may be able to increase your income by 40 to 50 percent though that is unlikely to happen while moving up in one company?

4. What are the guidelines for how much is reasonable? What is fair? Is it always reasonable to ask for more?

5. Read Matthew 20:1–15. How does this parable fit what you've learned?

6. What would you do if you tripled your current income? What could you offer that would merit that?

Do You Have
What It Takes?

*We were wild with joy because tomorrow
We would leave the known world behind.
What a wonderful feeling . . .
To be able to decide your own life and destiny
Obeying without limitations your own mysterious call,
And dreams and passions.*

—DOUCHAN GERSI

*Examine yourself; discover where your
True chance of greatness lies.
Seize that chance and let no power or
Persuasion deter you from your task.*

—SCHOOLMASTER IN *CHARIOTS OF FIRE*

*Create in you an irresistible energy,
Putting wings on your heart that will allow
You to fly beyond all self-imposed limitations.*

—GERALD JAMPOLSKY, M.D.

What if this whole process of looking for 1 more job leaves you cold? You still have trouble seeing the right fit in a company and the prospect of once again being vulnerable to the politics of a company doesn't exactly light you up. Maybe it's been awhile since you've had to do a job search or maybe the thought of having a boss half your age is not very appealing. Don't be discouraged! That in itself is part of this process of clarifying what does fit you. And you can choose the work that best fits you—work that fills you with excitement and passion every day. You really can have work that makes you want to get up in the morning; work that says, "This is why I was born!"

BEING THE BOSS
YOU ALWAYS WANTED TO HAVE

Maybe it's time to be your own boss—yes, to be the boss you always wanted to have. If you are a typical candidate for self-employment, you may never have been clear on what you wanted to do when you grew up. The traditional path may never have been appealing, and the attempt to be a good employee may have always been frustrating. Don't despair! Perhaps you just need a new work model. Even if you thought you knew where you were going, change may have hit you unexpectedly. Downsizings, outsourcings, and management adjustments may have forced you to take a fresh look at where you are and where you are going. Congratulations! Those very factors may just have offered you a new and better option.

> *"The problem with having a job is that it gets in the way of getting rich."*
> — Robert Kiyosaki
> Rich Dad, Poor Dad

Out of the frustration, discouragement, and intimidation, you may recognize excitement and hope just beyond the horizon. You may recognize that you have multiple areas of competence and that your years of working for companies has given you training in pretty much every aspect of running the company yourself. This may be your time to tweak the work model, giving you the time control and open-ended income you really want.

As you work through this process, be encouraged! There is hope! The options today are limitless. You really can be prepared, focused, and ready to move forward with the confidence and enthusiasm that project you into the next opportunity. I am not suggesting that you jump off a cliff, so to speak, bet the farm, or risk everything. Rather, I am suggesting that this may be a great time to explore all the new models for work that may give you a more true sense of accomplishment, meaning, service, and, ultimately, real security.

If you wanted to be an attorney with a large firm, an accountant with a Fortune 500 company, or a physician with a large metropolitan hospital, you would likely have enthusiastic audiences to cheer you on. Parents, teachers, college professors, and friends would encourage, prod, and guide you to success. If you were part of a top sales team or a computer programmer, you would be sent to regular industry seminars and training programs to build your skills and confidence.

But what if you are one of today's growing number of self-employed individuals? Then who cheers you on? Who guides you? Who tells you how to be successful and when to show up for work? Do your former coworkers, bosses, family, and friends

> *"The quality of the imagination is to flow and not to freeze."*
> *— Ralph Waldo Emerson*

encourage you, or do they think you are crazy to want to go out on your own? Do they admire your determination, or do they tell you that what you want to do is not practical or realistic? When problems arise, will they be sympathetic? After all, you chose to leave the *security, predictability, and stability* of a "real job."

In making the leap to being on your own, you may hesitate to discuss your concerns with those you know best. They have their own problems and pressures. Sometimes it's even hard to share your excitement as your success may remind them of their own misery at work. And can they really understand the merit of starting your own lawn maintenance service or dry-cleaning pick-up or senior day care or marketing your own art work?

Making the shift from a paycheck mentality to making it on your own can be exhilarating and intimidating at the same time. Pushing off from the shore without being able to see the desired port can seem to be a very risky proposition. Yet we know that in today's workplace, staying with a company can also be risky. Just recently I met with a gentleman, who after 32 years of faithful service with Texaco, was told his services were no longer needed. And at 57 years old, he was not ready or prepared to retire.

Another man at 46 years old, after 17 years of rising responsibility with Texas Instruments, was told he had 60 days to find something else to do. Did they think they had *security?* Certainly!

But what is *security*? General Douglas MacArthur defined *security* as "one's ability to produce." Your security is determined by your ability to define what it is you do that has value. The clearer you can be on what it is you do well and what provides value for someone else, the more security you have.

Security no longer comes from the company. Many people went to work for company giants like General Motors, AT&T, and Kodak, confident they would put in their appropriate time, and then be taken care of in the retirement years by these grateful companies. Those who went to work for nonprofit, government, or even parachurch organizations were even more confident. Surely these organizations would never downsize, lay off, or terminate their faithful servants. And yet we have seen hundreds of thousands from all of these companies, including the IRS, Christian record labels, and publishing companies, being eliminated with no clear solutions for their individual futures. Security has evaporated as it was historically understood.

Fortunately, technology has reduced the once-staggering cost of starting your own business to sometimes $0. So it doesn't matter that the banker isn't your brother-in-law because you aren't going to need $3 million to buy a bowling alley. Actually, technology has made it easy to run a 1- or 2-person business from home that even has the appearance of being a big business. I personally have more product sales than many traditional bookstores, yet I have no buildings, no leases, no sign permits, no employees, no worker's compensation, and little day-to-day inventory. Our products are distributed to a national customer base and many of the products we deliver are sent digitally, with no printing, no packaging, and no postage.

Keep in mind the biggest attraction of a self-owned business is not the money; it is the freedom—the chance to control your own destiny. A self-owned business can be the lowest-risk and highest-opportunity option for getting that control of your own destiny. With current technology and the multiple options in the workplace, you can start almost any business part-time and out of your spare bedroom.

Need Extra Income? Grab Some Fireflies

I often work with people in showing them how to create additional income without leaving their current job. Here's one idea I have never suggested until now.

Fireflies are used in some apparently very important research in molecular biology. Using firefly materials, scientists perform genetic research to find potentially revolutionary treatments for Alzheimer's and certain forms of cancer. Already there are promising developments in the treatment of Parkinson's and Huntington's diseases.

They will pay for fresh supplies of fireflies—33 cents per gram or $9.50 per ounce. This turns out to be approximately $1.30 per 100 fireflies caught. You do have to keep them dry and frozen and send them in quickly, but Kelly Smith of Lawrenceburg, Tennessee, scooped in 408 grams last year to earn a check for $129.

Let's see—the mortgage is due and the groceries are a little low. Or how about that new washing machine for only $399? If you can catch 30,692 fireflies, you can surprise your wife with that new washing machine.

For further information or questions, you can write to Firefly Project, 103 Wiltshire Drive, Oak Ridge, Tennessee 37830.

Incidentally, I do think there are better ideas for generating additional income.

Do You Have What It Takes?

Do you have what it takes to make your business successful?

Over the years, I have identified a number of traits that indicate a person's success in his or her own business. The more "yes" answers you have to the questions below, the more likely you have what it takes to run your own business. Each of the 18 questions is followed by a statement of why that particular trait is important.

_____ 1. Are you a self-starter? Successful business owners are always making things happen. They don't wait around for the phone to ring or to be told what to do next.

___ 2. Do you get along with different kinds of people? Every business, even small ones, requires contact with a variety of people: customers, suppliers, bankers, printers, etc.

___ 3. Do you have a positive outlook? Optimism and a sense of humor are critical factors for success. You have to view setbacks and small failures as stepping stones to your eventual success.

___ 4. Are you able to make decisions? Procrastination is the main obstacle to good decision-making. In a successful business, important decisions are made on a daily basis not put off. Eighty percent of decisions should be made right away.

___ 5. Are you able to accept responsibility? If you typically blame others, the company, the government, or your spouse for what goes wrong, you are probably a poor candidate for running your own business. Successful business owners accept responsibility for results even if those results are not favorable.

___ 6. Do you enjoy competition? You don't have to be cutthroat, but you must enjoy the thrill of competition. You must have a strong desire to compete, even against your own accomplishments of yesterday.

___ 7. Do you have willpower and self-discipline? Self-discipline is the one key characteristic that makes all these others work. Without it you will not succeed.

___ 8. Do you plan ahead? Every successful businessperson develops a long-term perspective. Going into business with a detailed plan dramatically increases the likelihood of business success. If you are already a goal-setter, you are more likely to succeed on your own.

___ 9. Can you take advice from others? Being in your own business does not mean you have all the answers. Being open to the wisdom and experience of others is the hallmark of a leader. People who are willing to listen spend more time doing what works the first time, rather than having to experience every mistake.

___ 10. Are you adaptable to changing conditions? Change is constant in today's marketplace. In every change there are the seeds of opportunity, thus successful people view change as an opportunity not as a threat.

____ 11. Can you stick with it? Most new ventures do not take off as quickly as we would like. Are you prepared to make at least a 1-year commitment to this business no matter how bleak it may look at times? Will you continue even if your friends tell you to throw in the towel?

____ 12. Do you have a high level of confidence and belief in what you are doing? This is no time for doubt or second thoughts. You must absolutely believe in what you are doing. If you don't have total belief, you will not be able to sell the idea, product, or service to investors or customers. Don't deceive yourself into thinking that you can do well something you don't really believe in.

____ 13. Do you enjoy what you are going to do? Don't ever think you can be successful doing something just for monetary rewards. Ultimately, you must get a sense of meaning and satisfaction from what you are doing. So only consider those ideas about which you are totally passionate.

____ 14. Can you sell yourself and your ideas? Many people fail with a great product or service because they can't sell. Nobody will beat a path to your door even if you do have a better mousetrap. Those days are gone. You will need to sell constantly.

____ 15. Are you prepared to work long hours? Few businesses are immediately successful. Most require months or years of long hours to get them going. It's like getting a plane off the ground. A great deal of energy is required at first, but once you are in the air, it takes less energy to keep moving. Businesses are very much the same.

____ 16. Do you have the physical and emotional energy to run a business? Operating your own business can be more draining than working for someone else because you have to make all the decisions and probably do all the work (initially, at least).

_____ 17. Do you have the support of your family and/or spouse? Without support at home, your chances of success are dramatically reduced. Doubt and misgivings can too easily creep in.

_____ 18. Are you willing to risk your money in this venture? If you are not, you probably question your confidence in the venture and your commitment to it. No bank or outside lender will be willing to take risk that you are not willing to back with everything you have.

More and more Americans are looking for greater control of their destinies and for the freedom that having their own business allows. Make sure you match your personal skills with the proper business choice. Your work must integrate your skills, your personality tendencies, and your interests. That may seem simple and obvious, but it is amazing how often those principles are violated. The more you know and understand about yourself and match that up with your business direction, the more you exponentially increase your chances for success.

Accidental Entrepreneur

Out of the ranks of the unemployed comes a new breed of self-starter: the "accidental entrepreneur"—someone who never imagined having his own business until there seemed to be no other option. I have seen airline pilots, physicians, human resource directors, CEOs, pastors, and attorneys who have lost their jobs. A music industry executive lost his job 4 times in the last 3 years. What are the chances of replacing that $130,000 per year position with a similar one? It's still possible but the odds are not great. And the odds for "security" and "predictability" have essentially disappeared.

But out of chaos and uncertainty, creativity is frequently born. A CEO is now a Web site writer, a pastor is now an artist, an attorney is developing an executive training seminar, and an airline pilot now has his own cruise agency. All claim an increased sense of control and freedom. Maybe your disaster is actually God helping you find your wings.

ARE YOU A CANDIDATE?

If you do think and make decisions like an employee, being on your own becomes an agonizing experience. Customers don't buy when they've indicated they will, equipment breaks when you least expect it, workers don't show up as planned, and the landlord raises the rent unexpectedly. In many ways, the characteristics that make a person a good employee are often the exact opposite of those that make a successful self-employed individual. Being loyal, predictable, and doing what others expect may, in fact, sabotage your best entrepreneurial efforts.

Much of the standard business methods may not apply to what you are trying to do. Bill Gates, Steve Jobs, Ross Perot, and Sam Walton did not follow standard business methods in building their companies. And for your business, workers compensation, lease agreements, and complicated accounting practices may have little relevance. Traditional knowledge of business plans and principles may not address the needs of today's freelancers, home-based business people, craftsmen, artists, writers, consultants, and contract workers whose numbers are exploding.

Even the traditional predictors (intelligence and education) may not provide much correlation to success for the self-employed person. In his popular book *Emotional Intelligence,* Daniel Goleman states, "There are widespread exceptions to the rule that IQ predicts success—there are more exceptions than cases that fit the rule. At best, IQ contributes about 20 percent to the factors that determine life success, which leaves 80 percent to other forces." He goes on to describe these *other forces* as "emotional intelligence": "abilities such as being able to motivate [yourself] and persist in the face of frustrations; to control impulse and delay gratification; to regulate [your] moods and keep distress from swamping the ability to think; to empathize and hope." These other forces—the 80 percent determinants of success—also include attitude, enthusiasm, energy, and tone of voice.

Richard Branson, the flamboyant billionaire founder of the Virgin empire (which encompasses over 150 businesses) was a dyslexic, academically struggling kid who did poorly on any IQ test. However, at age 17, while still in boarding school, Branson published an innovative newspaper called *Student*. He solicited corporate advertisers, linked students across schools, and filled the paper with articles written by rock stars, movie celebrities, and ministers of British Parliament. It was a huge business and financial success. The headmaster of his boarding school summed it up like this: "Congratulations, Branson. I predict that you will either go to prison or become a millionaire." Not a bad way for a guy who couldn't read well.

> "If one advances confidently in the direction of his dreams, and endeavors to live the life which he has imagined, he will meet with a success unexpected in common hours."
> — Henry David Thoreau

My friend Cindy Cashman is recognized as perhaps the most successful self-published author in the United States. At 23 years old, she was classified as illiterate. Her first book was titled *Everything Men Know about Women*. She published it herself and sold more than 1.3 million copies at $3.95 each. (I might add that it was 128 blank pages.) Her ability to see beyond the obvious allowed her to succeed in a writer's world as a person who struggled with reading herself.

▶ Multilevel Baloney

If you live in America, you have probably been approached by someone attempting to get you into a multilevel marketing (MLM) company. You know the routine: Buy this stuff, describe it to 3 of your friends, who incidentally will beg you for it because this is the revolutionary pill everyone has been waiting for, and in 6 months you will be making $20,000 a month and never have to work again. Many people are looking for more control in their lives and time and MLM offers that. But just as there are a lot of mismatches in regular jobs, there are many mismatches in the MLM arena. And here's the primary reason: Most multilevel marketing companies are promoting a fundamental falsehood—that anyone can be a great salesperson with the right tapes or coaching. That is absolutely false. Most people will never be good enough at selling to make a living at it, especially the nose-to-nose selling required in MLM. And no, it can't be done on the Internet. To succeed in MLM you need to connect with people and have an ability to handle rejection. Most people don't.

The success of the few comes at the expense of all the other people who waste their time and money pursuing a goal they can never reach. And that's my problem with 99 percent of multilevel companies: you are encouraged to make money on your ability to use other people.

Selling is an honorable profession. If you can sell, you can provide a valuable service to your customers, taking advantage of no one in the process. Be cautious of companies that provide 1 solution to everyone's dreams. Have you been interviewed as a reasonable candidate for what is required, or have you just been recruited as one more number in someone else's "downline"? If you are building your own MLM business, would you hire Uncle Fred as a salesman?

If you are involved with a MLM company, make sure you are doing it with the same integrity you would expect from any other business.

The downsizing of corporate America and the accompanying insecurity have fueled a resurgence of nontraditional work. These factors have also prompted the concept of having a core career, in which a person has a job that keeps a roof overhead and food on the table but also has 1 or 2 other profit-producing ideas in place as well. With the exploding opportunities in home-based businesses, many Americans are finding that it makes more sense to use this model than to attempt to find the one right job that provides all their needs. One of the hottest terms for creating a work life today is "multiple streams of income." This term has been defined in the book by the same title by entrepreneur Robert Allen. You may have 2 or 3 things that are creating income for you, rather than only 1 all-important job.

I happen to have seven areas of income; all with no employees and none with the look of a traditional business. I coach people individually, I sell books and computerized profiles, have facilitators around the country teaching the *48 Days* material, write articles for magazines and Web sites, etc.

You may not see yourself as a typical entrepreneur or business owner. But in going through any transition you must recognize all the options for selecting work. It would be shortsighted to look for only a traditional job when that model is diminishing. Just be aware of the new work models and ways to apply your unique skills.

Currently, about 60 percent of American homes have a business operating within their walls. Based on current trends, that number will grow to 72 percent in the next 5 years. This does not mean that the home-based business provides all the income for that family. It also does not mean that this is just someone selling a little soap and bringing in an extra $100 a month. The average home-based business in 2003 generated a little over $52,000. More than 78 percent of all U.S. businesses have fewer than 10 people involved and many of those businesses are operated out of someone's home. Gone are the days of needing a business loan, a building commitment, employees, and a 5- to 7-year wait for profitability.

Entrepreneur magazine tells us that 69 percent of all businesses being started today require less than $10,000 to launch. Twenty-four percent require no money at all.

How the Invention Marketing Con Game Works

You've seen the late night TV ads or the promises in the back of a magazine: Patent, package, and sell your invention!

Misconception 1: National programs and magazines would never allow con artists to use their media for advertising.

Truth: National publications don't have the time or the expertise to check out every potential advertiser. And these advertisers may spend $60,000 a month on their ads, so the media looks the other way.

Misconception 2: The inventor receives a glossy presentation and eagerly submits his/her idea for a free review.

Truth: The information presented is designed to mislead the inventor by outright lying or presenting misleading half-truths. Testimonials are usually false. Shills are put in place to answer calls about past clients.

Misconception 3: The company calls and excitedly says they have never seen anything like your idea and they are sure it will be an instant success. Of course, you must pay certain fees to obtain a patent and marketing report. Their questions about you will determine the fees—usually ranging from $650 to $7,000.

Truth: All ideas are accepted by the company. I once had a client who had designed a vibration-resistant cigarette plug-in adapter. How many of these do you think could be sold? But the company presented him with numbers of vehicles with cigarette lighters and by selling to only a small percentage, he would be a millionaire.

Misconception 4: There is a step-up process as you go along and you need to turn in more money for a "report." Companies are already contacting the patent company about a supply of your product.

Truth: This is the hardest part to swallow: the inventor does actually get a patent, but it is worthless. Keep in mind, most patents are worth only the paper they are printed on. The Patent Office issues more than 100,000 patents each year, most of which are worthless. You may patent a square wooden wheel because it hasn't been done, but who's going to want to buy one? A young couple I worked with had sent in over $10,000 twice to these scam companies and will never see a penny return. One patent was for a plastic sheet insert to organize your canceled checks.

This is a very brief introduction to a very big industry. Stay away from invention marketing firms that advertise on radio and late-night TV. They're out to fatten their wallets and empty yours!

Brian Tracy, a nationally known sales and business consultant, says most of us have 3 or 4 ideas a year that would make us millionaires if we just did something with those ideas. But most dismiss the ideas as impractical, unrealistic, or too expensive or think that someone has probably already tried it. Thus we lose the opportunity to change our own success.

Opportunities in service businesses, telecommunications, computer and Internet options, and network marketing all provide some explosive new choices. Many of these erase the old requirements of just exchanging time for dollars. You may be accustomed to receiving $10 an hour or $37,000 a year as an exchange of *time* and *effort*. But how do you relate to the idea of using an Internet site to provide information and see the potential of bringing in $1,000 a day? Or what about a mail-order product for your gardening interest that produces hundreds of orders weekly, so that you are being compensated for *results* not time and effort?

Be aware of this change from a time-and-effort economy to a results-based economy. If you went into a buggy shop in 1896 and ordered a small wagon, you would not have guaranteed that craftsman $10 an hour or agreed that he would receive $37,000 annually. Rather, you would have agreed on a set price for the finished product—let's say $100 for a finished wagon. Now, whether it took that craftsman 15 hours or 200 hours was not your concern; you simply paid for the completed wagon. This is a model based on results not time and effort. What we are seeing in our current work environment is a return to that simple model.

Even companies are beginning to say, "We will not guarantee payment just because you showed up for work; rather we will compensate you based on the production completed." A recent contract at Saturn in Spring Hill, Tennessee, included this concept. The employees there are being paid an agreed-upon base pay but receive their real bonuses based on the profitability of the company. This is a healthy return to a realistic method of compensation.

It may be necessary or advantageous for you to consider the unusual or unique as you explore new work opportunities. You could work for a sign company and be paid $15 an hour. But would you be willing to work for that same sign company and be paid $6 for every real estate sign you could paint this week? Or what about mowing yards at $65 each? Or advertising a family recipe in the back of a cooking magazine where you receive $3 for each order? If you are willing to look at new models, it will greatly expand opportunities for you.

A recent client, though he has advanced academic degrees, greatly enjoys the challenges of removing moles from people's yards. We are now developing a prototype for that business, which has all the possibilities of growing into a successful franchise business. *Watch for the Molenator!* (For free articles on non-traditional work, and to subscribe to a free weekly newsletter, go to www.48Days.com.)

Amish Business

In driving through Holmes County, Ohio, recently, I was again intrigued by the quantity of businesses operating in that Amish area. We watched 18-wheelers turn down tiny gravel roads to get to the various businesses tucked among the back roads. The diminishing number of people directly involved in agriculture has effected even this agrarian group. Reports indicate that in this community, more than half the Amish have left the farms to work in small businesses.

According to commerce information, there are about 1,000 Amish microenterprises in this area. Many of these boast annual sales of more than $500,000. Yes, employees are making buggies, harnesses, and lumber, but also furniture, modern cabinets, garage doors, and cheese. Restaurants, hotels, fitness centers, and tourists sites are flourishing. This is significant because of the trend toward small businesses and home-based businesses in the general population.

Yet, while the national failure rate for small businesses is listed as about 85 percent in the first 5 years, for these Amish businesses, the failure rate is less than 5 percent. How is it possible that these Amish entrepreneurs, despite having only an 8th-grade education—many with no technological advancements such as computers or even telephones and electricity—have such an astounding rate of success?

The researchers who have studied this phenomenon have identified 5 basic characteristics of these simple yet successful businesses:

1. *An ethic of hard work.* Proverbs 10:4–5 tell us, "Idle hands make one poor, but diligent hands bring riches. The son who gathers during summer is prudent; the son who sleeps during harvest is disgraceful."

2. *Use of apprenticeships to train young entrepreneurs.* We have lost the art of mentoring; Jewish fathers always taught their children a trade or skill. Today we are raising sons and daughters with no identifiable areas of vocational focus.

3. *Use of small-scale operations.* We are so quick to believe that bigger is better. Often it is just bigger.

4. *Frugality and austerity, resulting in low overhead.* In these Amish businesses, the owner is usually doing the hands-on work. No fancy offices or board rooms—just the basic needs. Operating from a home farm, many have no rent or lease expense.

5. *Product quality, uniqueness, and value.* The United States is known for shoddy workmanship and poor quality. A return to quality is a key to success. People expect Amish workmanship to be of high-quality, and they get what they expect.

These amazing results appear to be based on simple, basic principles. Integrity, character, and value do have a lasting and profitable outcome.

For a complete workbook process on starting your own successful business, see *48 Days to Creative Income* at 48days.com/products.php.

SOME IDEAS FOR SUCCESSFUL NONTRADITIONAL BUSINESSES

FRANCHISES

This is perhaps the hottest form of new business. For a franchise fee, you can purchase a proven concept for your business. Success rates are very high. You typically pay a percentage of all revenues as a franchise "royalty." Franchises range from expensive ($500,000) to very inexpensive ($595). This is not only for McDonald's or Subway. There are franchises for every concept you can imagine. A client of mine recently purchased a $10,000 cruise franchise that he and his wife operate out of their home. In the first 90 days, they booked over $100,000 in cruise packages, netting them 16 percent or $16,000. With that they recaptured all their expenses and began a very profitable and enjoyable self-owned business. (Check out the options at www.franchise.com or www.franchisehandbook.com/index.asp.)

BUSINESS OPPORTUNITIES

These are other forms of purchasing a concept, but they are not as heavily regulated as franchises, so do enough checking to feel comfortable with your choice. But you get a proven model for the business, usually a start-up manual, and some initial help from the parent company. From then on you are on your own but do not have to pay any ongoing monthly royalties like with a franchise. Business opportunities you may have heard of are Merry Maids, Merle Norman Cosmetics, Liberty Tax Services, ServiceMaster, and Furniture Medic. For more information, pick up magazines like *Entrepreneur, Business Start-Ups,* and many others. Browse through them at your local grocery store. Don't assume all these ideas are scams or rip-offs. You learn by gathering lots of information. Then you can recognize an idea that is valid and fits you.

LICENSING

You can sell NASCAR T-shirts or Tiger Woods golf clubs, but you will need to pay a licensing fee for using a well-known name.

However, you get to use the marketing power of a recognized name for a faster start. If you are simply purchasing shirts, mugs, banners, and so forth from an established manufacturer, the licensing issue has already been addressed and you can just focus on ways to generate sales.

DISTRIBUTORSHIPS

These are usually received just by asking the manufacturer or publishing company. For example, I am a distributor for several publishing companies. I purchase their book titles at a 50 percent discount and also look for overruns and remainders in books that I can purchase at deep discounts of 90 to 95 percent, to increase my margins. If you like garden tools, sports equipment, golf accessories, or pet products, you can often just ask for the distributor agreement.

HOME-BASED BUSINESSES

You may initially purchase a small inventory and be provided a little training, but for the most part you are on your own. The positives are that the cost is usually very low and you have no ongoing fees to the company that you purchased from. See an example at www.smcorp.com.

And here are some more ideas for things you can do on your own:

Accounting	Wedding planning
Personal servicing	Senior citizen caring
Portrait painting	Wedding photographing
Graphic designing	Computer consulting
Making gift baskets	Newsletter writing
Vending	Delivery servicing
Interior decorating	Flea market vending
Landscape designing	Home inspecting
Ceiling fans	Import/export brokering
House painting	Auto detailing
Selling used cars	Glass tinting
Child security systems	Power washing

Nutrition counseling

Growing wild herbs

One-person performing

Catering

Organic gardening

Tour guiding

Tree removing

Chimney cleaning

Building decks and coverings

College scholarship searching

Home schooling counseling

Manners instructing

Mail ordering

Balloon vending

Pet sitting

Real estate photographing

Aerial photographing

Discount coupon book

Internet marketing

  compiling

Designing how-to brochures

Add your own ideas to this list. Search the back classified ads in magazines like *Entrepreneur, Business Start-Ups, Income Opportunities,* and more.

_____   _____

_____   _____

▶ Work-At-Home Scams

You've seen the ads in the newspaper, on telephone poles, in your e-mail—"MAKE $1,000 A DAY!" I just received one: "30 DAYS TO A MILLIONAIRE—GUARANTEED!" Others claim, "NO EXPERIENCE NECESSARY! LIVE THE HIGH LIFE!" But as the saying goes, "If it sounds too good to be true, it probably is." I continue to hear from people who sent in their $30 for the instructions or went to the $89 seminar or even paid for the $3,500 computer training to guarantee their success. As people desire new options to the 8-to-5 grind, they are left vulnerable to scams.

Here are some ways to spot a scam:

- If the ad has a lot of CAPITALIZATION and EXCLAMATION POINTS!!!!!!!!!, warning signs should go off in your head.
- If they say you can make a lot of money with little or no work, don't believe it.
- If the ad is not clear and does not give details, you are being baited.
- If you have to call a 900-number for more information, you're being scammed.

Home employment schemes are among the oldest kinds of classified advertising fraud. Many require that you pay for instructions, training, or materials before any supposed profits. Envelope stuffing, assembly or craft work, and at-home training to make money are some of the most common scams.

If you suspect a scam, contact your local Better Business Bureau. They are very aggressive about stopping scams. Check out the Federal Trade Commission Web site for more information on avoiding and reporting scams (www.ftc.gov/bcp/conline/pubs/invest/homewrk.htm).

FREQUENTLY ASKED BUSINESS START-UP QUESTIONS

1. *What is the attraction to start-up entrepreneurial businesses?* More and more Americans are looking for greater control of their destinies and for the chance to apply personal skills to earn income. Most people are not as interested in material wealth as they are in time freedom. More than 800,000 Americans are starting their own businesses each year, and that annual number is growing.

2. *What are the key ingredients for success?* The ability to plan, organize, and communicate. And remember, 85 percent of your success will originate from your people skills—attitude, enthusiasm, self-discipline—and only 15 percent will be due to your technical skills.

3. *Don't most new businesses fail?* Once upon a time, someone churned out the statistic that 4 out of 5 small businesses fail in their first 5 years of operation. No one can trace the source of this mysterious figure, and not only is it illogical but also totally untrue. According to a Dun & Bradstreet census of 250,000 businesses, almost 70 percent of all firms were still around 12 years after startup. The study pinpointed the true failure rate at less than 1 percent of all businesses per year ("Business Beat," *Entrepreneur* magazine, July 2002).

Currently, we are gathering new information that helps us

understand the information about businesses staying in business. Knowing the characteristics of entrepreneurs, we know they often simply choose to discontinue one business and go on to a new one. That does not mean the old business was not successful or profitable; they just chose to go on to a new venture.

4. *Will we really see more and more small businesses?* Many of you have already experienced the downsizing of large corporations. IBM, General Motors, and other American standards have cut their workforces dramatically. The most recent U.S. Department of Labor's Bureau of Labor Statistics (www.bls.gov) show that in the period from July 2002 to July 2004 there were 3,947,342 initial claimants for unemployment, or 164,472 each month. The good news is that since 1982, the number of small businesses has grown by 50 percent to approximately 24.5 million. In the last 10 years, small business has accounted for 71 percent of the nation's new job growth, now adding more than 2 million new jobs each year. Small businesses employ 54 percent of the American workforce. What we are seeing is a healthy return to the kind of business that our country was founded on.

> *"Nothing splendid has ever been achieved except by those who dared believe that something inside them was superior to circumstance."*
> — *Bruce Barton*

5. *Are there any new ideas left?* Again, experts estimate that more than 85 percent of the products and services that we use today will be obsolete in 5 years. The airplane, tape recorder, artificial heart valve, soft contact lens, and personal computer were all new ideas in past years. With the changes we are experiencing in today's market, there are thousands of opportunities for new ideas. Keep in mind that today there are more than 5 million people working in Internet-related jobs. Ten years ago no one would have been able to foresee those opportunities.

6. *What if I'm not creative?* You don't have to be original to be successful in business. If you can do something 10 percent

better than it is currently being done or provide added value, you can be wildly successful. When Domino's got into the pizza business, it did not make better or cheaper pizza; it simply added delivery to a very common product. Meeting the desire for speed and convenience, Domino's created millionaires all across the country. Also, know that creativity is not a function of intelligence; rather it is a function of imagination. Have you ever known a child to not be imaginative? So are you. You may just need to tap into that childlike part of yourself once again.

7. *If I share my idea, will someone steal it?* Ideas are a dime a dozen. It's not even the quality of the idea but rather the quality of the action plan brought to that idea that determines success. Share your idea with others and get their input. Try your idea on friends and family. Make a prototype and see if people will buy it. Then gear up for a business supporting that idea. There is more to risk by not sharing your idea and getting input than there is in the slim chance that someone will steal your idea. Everyone is very busy with their own lives. It takes a lot of time and work to launch any idea. You are probably the only person with enough desire and ambition to actually carry it through.

8. *Should I buy a franchise, distributorship, or business opportunity?* The attraction of these options is that they are a tried system for a business concept. Normally, that means a proven track to run on, marketing support, and name recognition. But buyer beware: make sure you research carefully, so you don't overpay for something you could do yourself.

9. *Should I buy an existing business?* An average business costs $120,000—this will require $40,000 to 50,000 in a down payment and will typically provide a net income of $35,000 to 45,000. Plus, you will need some deep pockets for operating capital. This is not a very attractive proposition. Yes, there are good deals on existing businesses, but look carefully at why the business is being sold, and be clear on which tangible assets exist and which don't. Service-, Internet-, or home-based busi-

nesses are more difficult to value and may not have much in the way of real assets at all. You may be able to start with just an idea and build your own business.

10. *Is there one characteristic that is central to business success?* Yes, the ability to sell. Where there is no ability to sell, even the finest product or service business will fail. Fortunately, in today's marketplace, that does not mean you have to become a Donald Trump or Ted Turner to be successful. You can match the selling model with what you know about yourself. You can develop a method of selling that may never require you to talk to a customer, but you must have a system for selling or you will not survive.

COUNTDOWN TO WORK I LOVE

1. What do you think of the word *entrepreneur?*
2. Do you have what it takes to be on your own?
3. Are you an "accidental" entrepreneur?
4. What service or product could you promote?
5. What invention could you develop?
6. What are 3 or 4 ideas you have had over the years that you have on the back burner or have since seen someone else develop?
7. Describe 3 or 4 times in your own work experience when you have been paid on *results* or on completion of the job rather than just for putting in your *time.*
8. What would prevent you from doing something on your own?
9. Is it exciting or frightening to think about being your own boss?

Skunks, Rags, and Candy Bars

One day, the mother of future Microsoft mogul Bill Gates walked in on her young son to find him sitting there doing nothing. She asked Bill what he was doing. "I'm thinking, Mom, I'm thinking."

—WALTER ISAACSON, "IN SEARCH OF
THE REAL BILL GATES"

You can't use up creativity.
The more you use, the more you have.
Sadly, too often creativity is
Smothered rather than nurtured.
There has to be a climate in which
New ways of thinking, perceiving,
Questioning are encouraged.

—MAYA ANGELOU

What I lack is to be clear in my mind
what I am to do, not what I am to know . . .
The thing is to understand myself,
to see what God really wishes me to do . . .
To find the idea
for which I can live and die.

—SOREN KIERKEGAARD

Often times of change can help us see new opportunities. Joanne and I recently moved to a new place in the country. We love the quiet, the solitude, and the natural surroundings. However, we discovered that part of those natural surroundings includes nightly visits from a couple of skunks who took up residence under our house. Their chosen gift for us was a stench that came close to prompting us to visit the local Holiday Inn. Upon researching options to see who was going to remain occupants of the house, we were referred to "All Paws," a business run by a young man named John who removes any pawed animal. John came to our house and set the traps up to transport our little friends to a new home. And then by creating some wire mesh obstacles, he can discourage the little rascals from hanging around anymore. (Incidentally, John is a musician with a well-known country singer. This is just his means of making consistent income.)

> *"He who rejects change is the architect of decay. The only human institution which rejects progress is the cemetery."*
> — *Harold Wilson*

What a novel business idea! John sets the traps up for $55 and then collects another $50 for every animal trapped and removed. He told me he normally has 15 to 20 traps set, collects 4 to 5 animals and he's finished by 9:00 A.M. You can probably do the math on that. If he had a job paying $15 an hour he would have to put in approximately 65 hours a week to duplicate this income. Obviously, that wouldn't leave much time for guitar playing. As with most great business ideas, this is not new and revolutionary. It's a simple idea but done by someone who just did something!

THE TIMES, THEY ARE A-CHANGIN'

In 1970, Alvin Toffler wrote the popular book *Future Shock,* the landmark work about the effects of change on society. Toffler predicted that "millions of ordinary, psychologically normal people will face an abrupt collision with the future . . . many of them will find it increasingly painful to keep up with the incessant demand for change that characterizes our time."

Toffler's predictions have been strikingly accurate. Peter Drucker says we are in a 40-year period (from 1970 to 2010) that will see more change than the world has ever seen. As we approach the end of this time frame the speed of change will increase. We are rapidly approaching the time when 50 percent of all jobs will be contract or contingency labor. These are not the characteristics of the workplace we were led to expect by our parents and grandparents.

Instead, millions of Americans have found this new future shocking and unexpected.

THE FUTURE IS HERE

The victims of the wave of change are not hard to find. They are the 179,000 bank tellers who have been replaced by ATMs, the 47,000 postal workers replaced by sight-recognition machines, the 6,000 phone operators replaced by voice-recognition technology, and the grocery check-out clerks who have seen self-scanning systems replace them. They include the 334,000 steel and autoworkers and the 380,000 apparel workers who have seen their jobs go to other countries. Change of all types—economic, social, cultural, technological, and political—is occurring at an increasing rate.

> *"Show me a thoroughly satisfied man and I will show you a failure. I believe that restlessness is discontent, and discontent is merely the first necessity of progress."*
> — *Thomas Edison*

SEIZING THE OPPORTUNITIES

And yet, the world has always known change. At one point in American history, approximately 79 percent of our country's workers were directly involved in the production of agriculture. Today that number is less than 3 percent. Where have the other 76 percent gone? When an Eli Whitney invents the cotton gin, where do the farm workers who have been replaced go? When a robot replaces 16 men on an assembly line, where do these workers go? Are they really displaced to unemployment or unfulfilling lives, or can that displacement stimulate a transition to a higher, more fulfilling level of success?

We have seen these changes and transformations as we have moved from the agricultural age to the industrial age to the technological age and now the age of service and information. With each change, there are the seeds of new opportunities. That is one of the basic tenets of Napoleon Hill's classic book *Think and Grow Rich*—"With every change, there are the equal seeds of opportunity."

Like always before in our history, we need creative people to see the needs, to see the opportunities instead of the obstacles, and to create the future. It's bad enough for the secular world to be confused, but surely those of us with godly insight and principles at our disposal should have more clarity of direction. And yet we know that today, like at every stage of our country's development, the best opportunities may not look like those of yesterday. Today's best opportunities may not include punching a clock, having a company car, or being provided health insurance and a retirement plan. They may not involve an 8-to-5 schedule or even the need to go to an office.

> *"Life belongs to the living, and he who lives must be prepared for change."*
> *— Johann Wolfgang von Goethe*

STRETCHING YOUR THINKING

Many times in exploring new directions we are limited by our past experience. We tend to see boundaries that may not actually exist.

Here are a few mind teasers to help you think in unexpected ways (see answers at end of chapter).

- A bus with 15 passengers crashed and all but 9 people were killed. How many survivors were there?
- How many animals of each species did Moses take on the ark?
- I have 2 coins that total $.35 in value. One is not a quarter. What are the 2 coins?
- Mr. Jones was driving along the thruway with his son in the front seat. The road was icy. When Mr. Jones rounded a curve, his car skidded and rammed into a telephone pole. Mr. Jones was unhurt, but the boy broke several ribs. An ambulance took the boy to the nearest hospital. He was wheeled into the emergency operating

room. The surgeon took one look at the patient and said, "I can't operate on this boy. He's my son!" How could this be?

Sitting for Ideas

Henry Ford once said he didn't want executives who had to work all the time. He insisted that those who were always in a flurry of activity at their desks were not being the most productive. He wanted people who would clear their desks, prop their feet up, and dream some fresh dreams. His philosophy was that only he who has the luxury of time can originate a creative thought.

Wow! When's the last time your boss told you to quit working and do more dreaming? Unfortunately, our culture glamorizes being under pressure. Having too much to do with too little time is a badge of success. Or is it?

The apostle Paul took long walks between cities, using the time to think and talk. Andrew Carnegie would go into an empty room for hours at a time as he was "sitting for ideas."

> *"A mind once stretched, can never return to its original condition."*
> — *Oliver Wendell Holmes*

Thoreau wandered through the woods around Walden Pond, recognizing that the free time created fertile ground for original thinking. I grew up on a farm in Ohio where we got up at dawn and went to bed sometime after sunset. A change in the weather could create an unexpected time of leisure or dreaming. Neighbors had time to sit and talk and get to any appointments "directly," which could be in 10 minutes or a couple of hours.

If you are feeling stuck, your solution may not be in doing more, but in taking a break from the busyness of life. Try a little "sitting for ideas."

You really can love your work, but that may mean taking an active part in creating the work you love, rather than just looking around to see what jobs are available. Seizing new opportunities and responding to unwelcome change does not require settling for less. You can have a life full of adventure and satisfaction. Russian writer Maxim Gorky said, "When work is a pleasure, life is a joy! When work is a duty, life is slavery." Our work satisfaction impacts our life satisfaction. Happiness is loving what you do and knowing it is making a difference. If your life is not a joy, maybe it's time to look at some new options.

> *"The world hates change, yet it is the only thing that has brought progress."*
> — *Charles F. Kettering*

Joyce was frustrated in her work in medical sales. Five years earlier, she had invested all her money in opening a specialty bakery shop. Her unusual creations found immediate acceptance, and the customers flocked in as media coverage reached national business magazines. Eight months later she was bankrupt. Although people loved her tasty and appealing products, the details of running the business, complete with leases, sign permits, employees, and equipment purchases, proved to be too overwhelming. But that sense of "having something of my own" would not go away. Today Joyce has a small hot dog cart that she and her son operate. The entire purchase price was $3,800. She has exclusive rights to set up in front of the local Home Depot store on Fridays through Sundays. Joyce and her son enjoy the interaction with the many repeat retail and employee customers and take home a clear profit of approximately $1500 each weekend. She still has her job in medical sales. The solution was not an either/or but rather one of combining the benefits of both.

"Hold Fast to Dreams"

Langston Hughes was an African-American poet, novelist, and playwright, who became one of the foremost interpreters of racial relationships in the United States. Influenced by the Bible, W. E. B. Du Bois, and Walt Whitman, Hughes wrote poems in rhythmical language. His poems were meant "to be read aloud, crooned, shouted and sung." Why don't you try shouting this one? Go ahead! It'll do you good.

Hold onto dreams
For if dreams die
Life is like a broken-winged bird
That cannot fly.
Hold fast to dreams
For when dreams go
Life is a barren field
Frozen with snow.

HIGH-TECH HIGHS AND LOWS

In *The End of Work,* Jeremy Rifkin says the information age has arrived. In the years ahead, new, more sophisticated software technologies are going to bring civilization ever closer to a near-workerless world. The wholesale substitution of machines for people is going to force every nation to rethink the role of human beings in the social economy.

> *"Learn to pause . . .*
> *or nothing worthwhile*
> *will catch up to you."*
> — *Doug King, poet*

Theologian John M. Drescher tells the story about a corn farmer who won blue ribbons for his corn year after year. Yet each year he shared his best seed corn with all his neighbors. "How do you expect to continue to win blue ribbons," someone questioned him, "if you give your best seed corn to others?"

"You don't understand," said the farmer. "The wind carries the pollen from field to field. If I am to have the best corn, I must see to it that all my neighbors also have the best corn. If they produce poor corn, it will pollinate mine and pull my quality down."

So it is with all of life. We are all gardening the same plot of ground. The quality of our life has a direct bearing on the quality of our neighbor's life.

Innovation has always been a powerful force in our American culture. Automobiles, jet airplanes, air conditioning, telephones, and fax machines have eliminated distance and made the world a global village. We have seen these modern conveniences become seeming necessities. Who hasn't been reminded of the insidious penetration of modernity with the sound of a cell phone in Sunday school?

The modern worker, in an attempt to stay competitive, frequently makes available office, home, fax, and cell numbers, as well as 2 physical addresses for instant availability.

It is estimated that 1 week-day edition of today's *New York Times* contains more information than the average person in 17th-century England was likely to come across in an entire lifetime. Data has become more plentiful, faster (computer processing speed has doubled every 2 years for the last 30 years), and more frequent in presentation. In 1971 the average American was targeted by at least 560 daily advertising messages. Today, that number is more than 3,000 messages per day.

While we have always historically sought more information, we are now recognizing that too much information can make us anxious, less effective, and sometimes even sick. A new term, "data smog," has been invented for the noxious muck of the information age. Data smog gets in the way; it crowds out quiet moments and obstructs much-needed contemplation. It can spoil conversation, enjoyment of classic literature, and even simple entertainment, like family games and puzzles.

Nonetheless, the availability of information and the speed of change is not going to slow down; rather, it is going to increase. Are we being helped or victimized by this new information and these new inventions? Are they providing opportunities or prob-

"Playing it safe is like body surfing in two feet of water. You may not drown, but you're also not in deep enough to catch any but the most meager of waves. The most dangerous strategy is to play it safe. In its place, Break-It Thinkers take risks and break rules and challenge convention, making change an ally."
— *Robert Kriegel,* If It Ain't Broke . . . Break It!

lems? Is the Christian response to lead, follow, or get out of the way? Certainly, we have in each the proverbial glass of water, being either half full or half empty. I suggest that we be creators and yet not be controlled by the creations.

I operate a "virtual bookstore" for the *48 Days* products. We have no physical location, no building lease, no sign permits, no employees, and no hours of operation. Customers visit our "store" 168 hours a week and are free to browse while I am sleeping, traveling with my wife, or playing with my grandchildren. As a matter of fact, I tell people frequently that I'm quite fond of SWISS dollars—that's Sales While I Sleep Soundly.

> *"The world will never be happy until all men have the souls of an artist— I mean when they take pleasure in their jobs."*
> — *Auguste Rodin*

Every morning I take a quick look at the deposits that have been made into my bank account since I went to bed the night before. I don't have to be concerned about opening the store or whether there is 1 person, 50, or none in the store. I have no electric bill and don't need to make repairs to the shelves or walkways. I have no landlord and don't need to worry about bad weather conditions or street construction slowing sales. And while a traditional bookstore has about a 5-mile radius of customers, I have weekly customers in every state in the country as well as frequent ones around the world.

I only need a tiny fraction of the purchases of the potential market to do very well, while traditional bookstores are struggling more and more. Many of the products I deliver are e-books; that is, the customer pays for the book and then uses his printer and ink to get the purchased copy. I have no printing costs, no packaging, and no shipping charges. This is not a matter of right or wrong, good or bad; it's just a different way of doing business. Feel free to browse any time. Go ahead; you won't disturb me at all at www.48days.com/products.php.

Incidentally, we do ship lots of real books and CDs every day. Those are handled by a very competent stay-at-home mom. She works out of the bonus room in her lovely home, pulling the orders from the Internet, packaging the products, printing the UPS labels, and setting them aside for the daily pickup. If she needs to take a break, there is no time clock to check out, no boss to ask, and no interference with attending to her son. She frequently works in her pajamas, attending to our customers with care and consideration, but without the added expense or necessity of a fancy wardrobe. She spends no time commuting and has the liberty of working at 10:00 P.M. or 7:00 A.M. My business has grown dramatically through this kind of "strategic alliance" with professional service providers, who are located here in my community and around the country. It's a new way of doing business for all of us.

HIGH-TECH FOSTERS HIGH-TOUCH OPPORTUNITIES

A creative, responsive Christian increases in understanding and appreciation of new ideas, of other people, and of the world in general. A creative approach unlocks the mind and makes the spirit soar. God gives us creativity and ingenuity to make us feel *alive.* We should be leaders not victims, as the world becomes more complex and our societal problems become increasingly difficult to solve.

Our schools, families, churches, and communities are presenting us with critical new concerns that require new solutions. Many of these issues are suffering from a dearth of originality, and they need the creativity and spiritual insight of every maturing Christian. The solutions are not likely to be more information and more technology, but solutions that can only come from human touch and spiritual sensitivity.

Even in the career arena, you don't have to be a technological genius to survive and prosper. The U. S. Bureau of Labor Statistics forecasts 50 million new jobs opening up in the next 5 years with an explosion of opportunities for people who are *peacemakers, storytellers,* and *healers.* Fourteen of the 30 fastest-growing jobs in the next decade are for healers—and these are not only physicians and registered nurses. The number of certified massage therapists has quadrupled since 1990 as the 77 million baby boomers suffer an increasing burden of minor aches and tensions. The need for counseling therapists will grow dramatically as depression and major life changes confront these people entering the second half of their lives.

Universally, people are expressing more interest in spiritual matters, giving rise for directors of religious activities and education. More than 100,000 new jobs for clergy and religious directors are expected between 1996 and 2006.

The demand for simpler, more humane ways of resolving disputes will expand the opportunities for dispute mediation and arbitration. Ten years ago, there were about 150 dispute mediation centers nationwide; today, there are at least 500.

If God has gifted you to tell a good story, write a good book, or direct a good play, there will be opportunities for you.

David worked in a small newspaper office. But he really wanted to be a clown. Yes, a real red-nosed, big-shoed clown. In discussing the idea, I encouraged him to find something that would provide more continuity to the start-stop income he could expect from performing at special events only. Drawing on his writing background, he wrote a 24-page book titled *Mr. Tubby's Lemonade Stand.* He went to the local quick print shop and published his own book—a glossy cover stock with two staples in the middle. With that book in hand he scheduled himself for book signings at 8 area bookstores and filled his availability for birthday parties, festivals, and corporate events.

Then an unexpected thing happened. He was contacted by the national office of Junior Achievement. Unknown to David, the model Junior Achievement uses for teaching business and economic principles to high school kids is that of building and running a lemonade stand. Today he is a national spokesman for Junior Achievement, traveling around the country speaking and delivering thousands of copies of *Mr. Tubby's Lemonade Stand.* That's another example of starting with what you love and just taking small but definite action.

Myron began attending a weekly career seminar I was offering in Nashville, Tennessee. After several weeks he approached me with his frustration of feeling trapped and limited. He did not have a college degree and was stuck doing the only thing he had ever done—construction work. He was bored and tired of just working for someone else. He asked about going back to school to get computer training as that is where the opportunities were perceived. I questioned him about special areas of competence or enjoyment even in construction. He mentioned one thing that he did find enjoyable—a new process for stamping concrete to make it look like carefully laid stones. I asked him to come out to my house the next week.

When Myron arrived, I showed him an area where I wanted a curving sidewalk that came to our front door. I wanted a 5-foot-wide walk to curve around our planned waterfall. He got excited about solving every situation I presented and about how the finished product would look. Based on his excitement, I committed on the spot to have him do the job. As he had no start-up capital, I gave him half the money in advance for his initial materials. He worked hard in the creation of a beautiful curving walkway that immediately generated comments from clients and friends at our house.

From that simple start we were able to refer him several additional jobs and they did the same. He decided on the name, Lasting Impressions, and went on to generate well over $100,000 in sales in his first year of business. It's his business, he's doing what he loves, and it draws from all those years of working when he thought he was only making a living.

In the last few years I have seen a lady who personalizes candy bar wrappers, a young man who picks up dry cleaning from businesses, a couple who cut up flawed fabric into commercial rags, a fireman who services cologne vending machines on his off days, and a lady who makes great cheesecakes for local restaurants.

Most great business ideas are not new and revolutionary. They are simple but done by someone who just did something! A good idea will not put money in anybody's pocket, but combined with a plan of action that good idea can give you time control and unlimited income. For a business planning guide, just e-mail business@48Days.com.

COUNTDOWN TO WORK I LOVE

1. Who has launched a successful business after being fired at a previous job?
2. What unique skills do you have that may be the basis for a creative business (writing, drawing, building, analyzing, singing, driving, thinking, etc.)?
3. Do you have any ideas that would fall into the "peacemakers, storytellers, and healers" category?
4. Can you think of an idea that would create SWISS dollars for you?
5. Do you ever give yourself time to "sit for ideas"?
6. "Take delight in the LORD, and He will give you your heart's desires" (Ps. 37:4). How does this apply to being content in a job you hate?
7. How does your culture, environment, and experience perhaps limit your being able to see new opportunities?

Answers to Stretching Your Thinking
- All but 9 people were killed; thus there were 9 survivors—not 6!
- How many of each species did Moses take on the ark? Check your Bible. It wasn't Moses; it was Noah!
- The 2 coins are a dime and a quarter. Yes, I said 1 is not a quarter, and that's true: 1 is a dime not a quarter.
- The surgeon was the little boy's mother. Our assumption is that a surgeon is a man.

Conclusion

Years ago, when the first diamonds were being discovered in Africa, diamond fever spread across the continent like wildfire. Many people struck it rich in their search for the sparkling beauties, and they became millionaires overnight.

At this time, Lamar, a young farmer in central Africa, was scratching out a moderate living on the land he owned. However, the promise of great diamond wealth soon possessed Lamar, and one day he could no longer restrain his insatiable desire for diamonds and the lust to become a wealthy man. He sold his farm, packed a few essentials, and left his family in search of the magnificent stones.

His search was long and painful. He wandered throughout the African continent, fighting insects and wild beasts. Sleeping in the elements, fighting the damp and cold, Lamar searched day after day, week after week, but found no diamonds. He became sick, penniless, and utterly discouraged. He felt there was nothing more to live for, so he threw himself in a raging river and drowned.

Meanwhile, back on the farm Lamar had sold, the farmer who bought the land was working the soil one day and found a strange-looking stone in the small creek that ran across the farm. The farmer brought it into his farmhouse and placed it on the fireplace mantle as a curio.

Later, a visitor came to the farmer's home and noticed the unusual stone. He grasped the stone quickly and shouted excitedly at the farmer, "Do you know this is a diamond? It's one of the largest diamonds I've ever seen." Further investigation revealed that the entire farm was covered with magnificent diamonds. In fact, this farm turned out to be one of the richest and most productive diamond mines in the world, and the farmer became one of the wealthiest men in Africa. (Story from *The Speaker's Sourcebook* by Glenn Van Ekeren.)

How sad that Lamar had not taken the time to investigate what he had right at his own fingertips. Instead, he gave up everything he had in search of wealth that was right under his nose. The seeds of opportunity usually are in what we already know and are already doing. Don't think the grass is greener on the other side of the fence or that you must start something totally new and different to become successful.

I went to a funeral just yesterday. A 46-year-old client and friend was hit by an oncoming car on his way to work. He was still conscious when the ambulance crew arrived. The first thing he told them was that he didn't want to be late for work. Unfortunately, his internal injuries were such that he died about 5 hours later. His wife and children were with him and all got to say their last good-byes. At the funeral, stories were told of this man who lived and loved well. He loved his family and he loved his work. He told his children that he got paid to play. That fit in his work spilled over into his natural love of family, church, and community.

We tend to put the cart before the horse. Looking for the best opportunities in careers and jobs often leads to disillusionment and frustration. Look for what you love first. Then you will have the confidence and enthusiasm to find success in places others overlook.

Finding the work you love is an ongoing process. It's healthy at any given point to take a fresh look at who you are, where you're going, and how you're going to get there. It doesn't matter if you're 18 or 78. Recognize the value of circumstances and ongoing life experience. Uncertainty and frustration in a job or even losing a job can often simply be a prod to a higher level of success.

As I often relate, the eagles build a nest using thornbush strands to lock it together. Then they cover them with leaves and feathers to make it soft and comfortable. However, when the little eaglets are about 12 weeks old, the mom and dad eagles begin to remove the protection from the thorns. Pretty soon the little eaglets are up on the edge of the nest to avoid the pain and discomfort. Then the mom and dad eagle fly by with tasty morsels of food just out of reach. The little eaglet sees that if he leaves the nest, he'll drop and crash on the rocks below. However, as the discomfort continues the little eaglet makes a big leap to get away from the pain and toward the food and discovers he can fly. Oftentimes God allows circumstances in our lives not to leave us in pain and hunger but to lead us to higher levels of success that we would not otherwise explore. See the thorns in your situation as a prod to explore new options.

"Make no little plans; they have no magic to stir men's blood and probably themselves will not be realized. Make big plans; aim high in hope and work, remembering that a noble, logical diagram once recorded will not die."
— *Daniel Burnham, Chicago architect*

Do not look at any circumstances or past history with regret, but simply learn from them as you create a clear plan for the future. Everyone has events that have helped to make us what and where we are. You simply must look at where you are and then create a clear plan for the future you want. That process of seeing 5 years out and clarifying what you want that to be will immediately begin to lessen the uncertainty about any current situation.

As has been stated repeatedly, this is a very individualized process. Clarify what unique characteristics you bring to the table. Even when confronted with the realities of making a living, you still are not locked into repeating what you have done. God has equipped you with unique skills. Sort out the positives and expect to find applications that draw on your known abilities but also address the mission of your life. We want options that complement your multiple life goals—going beyond just job or career.

Understand your areas of strength and how they impact organizational focus and leadership. If you have great financial and administrative abilities, those should be explored as you look at possible new alternatives. If you have the ability to organize, plan, develop systems, and self-start projects, then embrace those in the selection process. Recognizing competence in technical, analytical, and detail skills can be integrated even if you are creating your own business. Those characteristics will help you create a sales/marketing model for your business that does not depend on nose-to-nose selling but, rather, on established systems. Your enjoyment of church involvement, your passion for photography, your desire to increase your income, and your desire to contribute to worthy and noble causes can all be considerations in identifying a new direction. (Remember Eric Liddle in *Chariots of Fire*—"God made me fast, and when I run I feel His pleasure.") Don't think this is a time to ignore your true passions even if the normal applications do not seem to produce the income results. And remember the story of the 10 talents. If you have the ability to increase your responsibilities and income and channel it wisely, then not doing so may be poor stewardship. Your desire to help, to serve people, to do something that lasts in people's lives, and to make a difference will all help in selecting the proper direction.

I love the symbolic characteristics of eagles. They are powerful, distinctive animals. Able to soar above the rest of the world, they could easily become content, unfocused, and lazy. And yet, they instinctively realize that to maintain pure survival, they must be aware and take the initiative for new methods, strategies, and information. We, as well, must follow their lead.

In today's rapidly changing environment, lack of growth will put a person in the back of the pack quickly. As previously mentioned, the second law of thermodynamics tells us that left to themselves things tend to deteriorate. Never has this law been more evident than today. Companies, individuals, and even churches not looking for innovative ways to do things are being left behind.

We are in the age of the knowledge worker where new learning is essential. Keep learning; don't end your education when you finish school. Degrees and training received 10 years ago may not be relevant today. Industries and technology that previously took 40 to 50 years to become outdated are now becoming obsolete in 4 to 5 years. Computers are replacing people, information is replacing technology, and results are replacing time and effort. Constant growth is an absolute requirement for simply maintaining a valued place in today's world.

Change is inevitable; how will you respond? You can choose to wring your hands as a victim, or use your God-given creativity to see where He is leading you. Each of us has been given unique skills, abilities, personality traits, values, dreams, and passions. We should be at the forefront as innovators and inventors, shining examples of excellence and accomplishment in all we do. Creating an individual path of mission and calling, we cannot then be victimized by any corporate downsizing or any other effects of future shock. Rather, we will seize the opportunities and lead the way to higher levels of fulfillment, income, and methods for blessing those around us.

After considering these options, you are ready to create your own 48-day plan! Check the appendix for additional help and then begin to work through the stages of your plan. You can do this. *You can achieve the success you are seeking.* Take inventory, focus, create a plan, and act.

COUNTDOWN TO WORK I LOVE

1. What action can you take in the next 48 hours to put you on the path for what you want to accomplish?
2. What idea have you gotten while on the beach or mowing your yard that could be worth more than a lifetime of hard work?
3. Are you a creation of circumstances or a creator of circumstances?
4. What seeds did you plant in your mind 5 years ago that brought you to where you are today?

Appendixes

Sample Résumés

(Use a format like this if you want the focus to be on skills rather than on employment locations.) Notice the skills are described without being pigeon-holed in any one industry. Company affiliations are de-emphasized. The focus is on areas of competence so that this candidate can change industries.

James Spencer
4598 Meadow Trace
Columbus, Ohio 44929
(419) 377-9845

SKILLS SUMMARY

Over 14 solid years of professional selling and sales management. Experienced in planning, organizing, and overseeing projects. Knowledgeable in hiring, training, and supervising. Team player in maintaining company policies and procedures. Committed to high work ethics and to attainment of management goals and objectives.

QUALIFICATIONS

ADMINISTRATION

Responsible for 21-person staff in current position. Increased gross revenues from $16.2M to $31.5M in 3-year period, while increasing pre-tax profit over 200 percent. Directed employee training and employee evaluations. Competent in dealing with compensation negotiation and conflict resolution. Able to handle variety of tasks and responsibilities simultaneously. Strong leadership skills and accountability to management. Provided valuable input for long-term planning and market assessment.

SALES

National Sales Manager of the Year. Closed largest commercial account in TN. Negotiated accounts with So. Central Bell and the new Columbus Arena. Closed first tier account program with 48 regional chain stores, involving in excess of $200K annually. Able to interact with key community and business leaders. Adept at recognizing customer needs and achieving balance between customer needs and company goals and policies. Personal commitment to integrity results in increased sales and customer confidence.

ORGANIZATIONAL SKILLS

Developed successful inside-marketing concept, which was given national rollout in 2001. Used TeleMagic software to establish pilot program, "Pricing for Profit," for 300 national offices. Designed palm-top computer usage for field representatives to streamline efficiency. Analyzed sales figures and business trends to increase sales.

PROFESSIONAL EXPERIENCE

BFI OF OHIO—COLUMBUS	—Columbus, OH	
Sales Manager	2001–Present	
WRIGHT INCORPORATED	—Worthington, OH	
Sales Manager	2000–2001	
ABC PRINTING, INC.	—Dayton, OH	
Sr. Account Manager	1994–2000	
ARC/AMS DIVISION OF AMERICAN EXPRESS	—Columbus, OH	
Sales Representative	1987–1994	

EDUCATION

OHIO STATE UNIVERSITY
Columbus, Ohio 1983–1987

CLUBS AND ORGANIZATIONS

Who's Who Among Students in American Colleges
and Universities
Big Brothers/Big Sisters—Board Member
Columbus Rotary Club
Columbus Chamber of Commerce

REFERENCES

Available upon request

This woman had only one employer, no college degree, and assumed she was trapped. But we emphasized transferable areas of competence, positioning her as a great candidate in other industries.

Joyce A. Parker
398 Manor View Lane
Brentwood, TN 37027
(615) 377-6798

SKILLS SUMMARY

Solid experience in multiple facets of office operations. Knowledgeable in data entry and computer functions. Proven skills in instructing and motivating coworkers. Committed to high work ethics and to attainment of management goals and objectives. Described by others as loyal, trustworthy, and fun-loving.

PROFESSIONAL EXPERIENCE
SOUTH CENTRAL BELL, Nashville, TN August 1983–Present

ORGANIZATION

Oversaw development and implementation of programs, switching from rural route numbers to house numbers. Increased efficiency of departmental system. Dealt with key community leaders to coordinate 911 system. Competent in technical areas with focus on detail and accuracy. Performed accounting functions including reconciling employee payroll records, data entry, and inventory management.

TRAINING

Confident in managing and supervising employees. Works well with all personality styles. Responsible for accuracy of incoming employee performance. Strong interpersonal skills with ability to diffuse workplace tension. Created departmental instruction manual. Coordinated employee hours and duties while building team spirit and commitment. Able to handle variety of tasks and responsibilities simultaneously. Strong accountability to management. Part of #1-rated office in 9-state region.

CUSTOMER SERVICE
Competent in setting up service and completing problem resolution. Assisted in negotiating customer concerns, leading to win-win solutions. Liaison between company and clients. Ability to communicate with customers in person or by telephone and to establish rapport and support.

EDUCATION

Nashville Technical Institute	—Beginning Electronic Telecommunications
Overton High School	—1983 Graduate

PROFESSIONAL SEMINARS

- *Be a People Pro*
- *Telecommunications Excellence*
- *Customer First Service*
- *The Quality Advantage*

REFERENCES
Available upon request

This writer has hands-on construction background but is moving into professional management.

Tom Phillips
187 Pepper Ridge Circle
Lakeland, Florida 23689
(863) 831-3587

SKILLS SUMMARY

Solid experience in management and supervision of construction field projects to completion. Possesses the skills to build, strengthen, and maintain people relationships. Excellent writing and verbal skills. Technical aptitude and background. Self-motivated in continuing education. Professional manner and personal commitment to high standards of integrity.

QUALIFICATIONS

MANAGEMENT

Accomplished in planning, scheduling, and directing construction projects to completion. On-site supervision of detailed homes valued up to $650,000. Assisted in planning for new upscale subdivision. Responsible for contractor-customer follow-up and liaison.

INTERPERSONAL SKILLS

Proven ability to interact positively with a wide range of people. Five years in field sales, selling premium-quality products and opening new accounts with follow-up, service, and repeat sales. Participated in field training of sales reps. Program included instructing, training, and evaluation with both trainees and home-office management. Won company-wide award for highest training sales production.

TECHNICAL ABILITY

Bachelor's degree in biology with chemistry minor. Resourceful in research and information searches. Self-taught in knowledge of selection and use of construction materials and structural requirements. Successful experience in understanding and operating within technical boundaries, focusing on detail and accuracy.

PROFESSIONAL EXPERIENCE

MAINTENANCE ENGINEERING—LAKELAND, FL
Sr. Field Trainer and Field Sales   May 1997–Present

ADEX CORPORATION—LAKELAND, FL
Superintendent of Construction   Jan. 1991–Nov. 1997

PRESERVATION CONSTRUCTION COMPANY—ATLANTA, GA
Superintendent of Construction   Mar. 1987–Jan. 1991

NAS CONSTRUCTION COMPANY—ORLANDO, FL
Owner operator   Mar. 1983–Mar. 1987

INTERNATIONAL HARVESTER COMPANY—ORLANDO, FL
Quality Control Inspector   1982–1983

EDUCATION

Florida State University—Gainesville, FL
Bachelor of Science—1981 Biology major; Chemistry minor
Dade County Vo-Tech
Building Trades—1975–1976

SEMINARS

Denis Waitley 1999
Brian Tracy
"Psychology of Success" July 1997
Media Images
Jan. 1989–Mar. 1996
Kenneth Blanchard
"The One Minute Manager" 1993
Adventure Works
"The 48 Hour Adventure" 1992

REFERENCES

Available upon request

This writer has technical construction skills and is building directly on past experience.

Bob Francis   *Résumé of Qualifications*
367 Old Hickory Blvd.
White House, Tennessee 37189 (615) 931-4507

SKILLS
SUMMARY   More than 24 years experience in construction, including management/supervision, estimating, and purchasing. Working knowledge of drafting, carpentry, and welding, with excellent troubleshooting and problem-solving skills.

PROFESSIONAL
EXPERIENCE   **FOREMOST CONSTRUCTION** Nashville, TN
               July 1998–Present
               Licensed Contractor #00036484

               HARDAWAY CONSTRUCTION Nashville, TN
               April 1995–July 1998
               Journeyman Carpenter

               MILLWORKS INTERNATIONAL Nashville, TN
               Feb. 1991–April 1995
               Manager: Estimating, Purchasing,
               Designing Cabinetry, Supervising
               cabinet makers.

               FLOUR DANIEL SERVICES CORP. Greenville, SC
               March 1990–May 1991
               Journeyman Carpenter: Read blueprints,
               shot elevations, operated manlifts,
               and supervised concrete pouring.

               FRANCIS CABINETS Joelton, TN
               Feb. 1984–March 1990
               Owner/Operator: Responsibilities
               included all sales, estimates,
               drafting, purchasing, and collecting.

HAURY & SMITH
CONSTRUCTION COMPANY Nashville, TN
Jan. 1983–Feb. 1984
Trim Carpenter

EDUCATION **TENNESSEE STATE UNIVERSITY** 1991–1994
NASHVILLE AREA VOCATIONAL SCHOOL
(Welding—496 Hrs.) (Architectural
Draftsman Detailer—676 Hrs.)

REFERENCES Available upon request

This writer is a sales professional, building from past employer experience.

WILLIAM W. BARNETTE, JR.
110 St. Andrews Drive
Rome, GA 37064
(713) 646-3274

SKILLS SUMMARY

Solid experience in consultative outside-selling, promoting, and concept marketing. Competent in planning, organizing, and creating strategic plans with distributors. Committed to high work-ethics and attainment of sales goals. Proven skills in territory management and the ability to increase sales. Comfortable negotiating agreements with win/win outcomes.

PROFESSIONAL EXPERIENCE

1985–Present **COOPER INDUSTRIES, INC. (CROUSE-HINDS ECM DIVISION)**

Sales Representative

Market-wide range of specialty products to Industrials, OEMs, and electrical contractors. Responsibilities include establishing product specifications with design engineers while generating increased sales. Coordinate market planning, product training meetings, stock analysis, and new product introductions. Budget has expanded 250 percent over 4 years to $2.5 million while budget goals have been achieved each year. Increased current territory sales by 25 percent. Promoted to Senior Sales in 1987.

1984–1985 **GENERAL ELECTRIC COMPANY**

Customer Service Representative

Coordinated inside sales responsibilities to OEM accounts representing 3 million in sales in 1984. Provided technical assistance, negotiated pricing, generated technical quotations in addition to scheduling sales orders.

1983–1984 **CHAMPION INTERNATIONAL, INC.**
      Sales Service Representative
      Sold forest products for Fortune 500 company
      through selected building materials distributors.
      Inside sales responsibilities included inventory
      control of satellite distribution center and pur-
      chase of selected products.

1981–1982 **B-LINE SYSTEMS, INC.**
      Outside Sales
      Promoted to outside sales after 8 months in terri-
      tory of North and South Carolina. Sold through
      electrical distributors. Responsible for product
      specifications at major industrial accounts and
      engineering firms.

EDUCATION B.S.—Georgia Institute of Technology, 1981
      Major: Industrial Management

REFERENCES Excellent references available upon request

This gentleman had been out of the workforce for 3 years with a triple organ transplant. We drew from competencies of work experience prior to that time, but were able to cover the gaps and move on.

James Bronson
3856 Confederation Rd.
Nashville, Tennessee 37229
(615) 896-3464

SKILLS SUMMARY

Solid engineering experience in machining and fabricating manufacturing environments. Strong interpersonal skills and ability to interact positively with all levels of management. Proven skills in technical design and systems, balanced with people-management ability. Committed to high work-ethics and to attainment of management goals and objectives.

RELEVANT SKILLS AND EXPERIENCE

MANAGEMENT

Capable of building strong teams for maximum use of people resources. Skilled at negotiating and resolving employee needs. Able to select, manage, and motivate people for efficient production. Served as liaison between engineering and manufacturing. Responsible for quality and schedule performance. Competent in assessing risk factors.

PROJECT COORDINATION

Implemented and installed CAD/CAM/CIM system. Responsible for government regulations and DOD testing requirements. Quite familiar with quality issues and requirements, including MIL-STD 9858, Ford's Q-101, and GM's Targets For Excellence. Oversaw purchasing, JIT, Kanban logic, statistical process control, time measurement, and inventory control. Proficient at job costing, quoting, and processing.

ENGINEERING

Designed flow of work for innovative engine design (Ford's MOD-3 Modular Engine). Facilitated machining changes and personally suggested improvements. Strong background in automotive engineering. Experienced with conventional machining, automatic screw machines, cold-forming, stamping, stretch-forming, CNC mills, and turning centers. Supervised and programmed CNC machined products relating to the fluid motion and fluid power industry, including hose fittings, connectors, and fasteners for the military, automotive, and OEM manufacturers.

PROFESSIONAL HISTORY

BLAIRS, INC. Nashville, TN 1997–Present

PARKER HANNIFIN CORPORATION Cleveland, OH 1990–1997

AVCO/TEXTRON AEROSTRUCTURES Nashville, TN 1987–1990

BETTY MACHINE CO. Nashville, TN 1985–1987

EDUCATION

B.S. Manufacturing Engineering Technology, MTSU, May 1995
A.S. Mechanical Engineering, July 1987
A.A. Industrial Engineering, March 1987
(Currently completing M.S. in Industrial Studies)

REFERENCES Available upon request

Note specifics in work history. The more specific you can be, the fewer the competitors, and the more likely you are to raise your salary range. You will also separate yourself from recent graduates, but also from those with perhaps more degrees and credentials.

Dorothy Newsom, P.E.
126 Riverwood Drive, Pittsburg, PA 24356
412-790-3487

PROFILE

Engineering/Project Management

Skills encompass engineering management, team leadership, and field project management. Background in industrial, commercial, petrochemical, and residential projects with involvement from concept development and initial client presentations through design/build to acceptance and preparation of proposed drawings. Extensive experience working with consultants (architectural, environmental, legal, governmental).

EXPERIENCE

SMITH AND WATSON, INC. Pittsburgh, PA 1996–Present
Principal Engineer
Selected Projects:

Field Engineer at Tooele, Utah, U.S. Army munitions storage plant. Resolved conflicts with design drawings and coordinated final design requirements. Provided detail for 100+ specially designed embedded wall plates that facilitated easy placement of concrete and expedited project.

Conducted inspections for ERMST (Earthquake Recovery Management Support Team) following the Northridge earthquake. Wrote reports for county, authorizing residential buildings to receive funds for reconstruction.

Conducted structural analysis using 3-D computer model for ARCO GHX-1 and GHX-2 steel-frame structures.

FLOUR-DANIEL/TRS, Philadelphia, PA   1988–1996
Civil/Structural Engineer

Managed FAA Golden Gate Airway Sector refurbishment project. Analyzed refurbishment needs for coming year and created and implemented site-specific solutions. Monitored annual budget of $9 million. Acted as liaison between field offices, site supervisors, and governmental agencies. Prepared budgets and cost estimates for projects and oversaw new construction.

Designed pre-engineered metal buildings for public, private, and commercial use.

Developed construction details that allowed metal-roof framing to accommodate masonry and tilt-up panel walls, significantly expanding product market and increasing sales.

BROWN AND LINSEY, Hershey, PA   1985–1988
Project Engineer

Lead structural engineer for creation on concrete and steel structures for refinery and chemical plants. Oversaw 4 engineers in pipe-support group. Constructed 3-D computer models to analyze various structures. Designed plant facilities and modification of existing facilities.

EDUCATION

UNIVERSITY OF TENNESSEE, Knoxville, TN
Bachelor of Science, Civil Engineering
CREDENTIALS
State of Pennsylvania Civil Engineer No. C03787345
State of Pennsylvania Structural Engineer No. S099743
AFFILIATIONS
Member, Structural Engineers Association of Pennsylvania
Pittsburgh Chamber of Commerce
Women in Business, National Association

REFERENCES
Available upon request

SAMPLE INTRODUCTION LETTER

The italicized headings below are not to be included on your letter but show you the issues to be addressed.

Mr. David C. Milton
BMI International, Inc.
7300 Franklin Road
Brentwood, TN 37027

Dear Mr. Milton:

Introduction: After more than 14 years as a sales professional in the medical

Current Situation/Goals: field, I am exploring new opportunities where my sales abilities may continue to be used. Positions commensurate with my past experience and career goals would be:

> Manager of Training and Staff Development
> Manager of Human Resource Development
> Director of Sales and Marketing

What's Special about Me: My record is one of solid accomplishments and increasing levels of responsibility. The training programs I have developed have been adopted as a model for our company's 23 nationwide locations. My sales goals have been exceeded by an average of 34 percent in the last 5 years.

Next Step: I will forward my résumé to you in the next few days to allow you to explore how my qualifications may match growth opportunities in your company.

Sincerely,

Jason L. Smith

Notice this requires nothing of the recipient. It simply tells him/her what is going to happen next. And it plants the seed so your name begins to become familiar. We are in a culture where repetition sells, and in this process you want at least 3 exposures to create "top of mind" positioning.

SAMPLE COVER LETTER

Kevin A. Smith
3736 Mitchell Drive
Ft. Collins, Colorado 76809

November 30, 2002

Mr. William Fowler
Vice President of Sales
The Dixon Company
199 Commerce Way
Boulder, Colorado 76821

Dear Mr. Fowler:

With this letter, I wish to express my strong interest in working with the Dixon Company as a regional sales manager. After 7 years in sales management and customer service, I believe I would bring several areas of competence to the Dixon Company. Accordingly, a complete résumé detailing my professional background is enclosed for your review and consideration.

In my current position, it is my responsibility to recruit, motivate, and train my staff to ensure that high quality and desired goals are obtained. In addition, I oversee the business development of all new products with bottom-line accountability for established profit goals. It is also my responsibility to maintain the integrity of the account base through sound credit decisions.

In this assignment, I opened a branch in a new market and doubled the account base in 6 months, reaching 150 percent of the expected growth and 200 percent of the profit goal. I accomplished this by leading the staff in effectively cross-selling our product line and providing exceptional customer service. This is just one example of how the Dixon Company may benefit by our mutual alliance.

I would very much like to speak with you about the sales management opportunities and ways that you can use my expertise.

Please expect my call on Wednesday, December 7, to arrange a convenient time to discuss that and more. I look forward to speaking with you then about opportunities in the Southwestern or Midwestern U.S.

Sincerely,

Kevin A. Smith
kas
Enclosure

You'll notice it does not say, "I look forward to hearing from you" or "Please call me at your earliest convenience." You must stay in the driver's seat.

Sample Follow-Up Letter

Charles S. Miller
2503 Concord Lane
Lakeland, Florida 27064
(863) 453-7786

James R. Johnson
Executive Director, YMCA
Orlando, Florida 26459

Dear Mr. Johnson:

Thank you for the opportunity to interview for the Youth Development Coordinator position. I appreciate your consideration and interest in me.

As we discussed this afternoon, my experience and educational experience have prepared me well for this position. I have enjoyed the similar work I have been privileged to do both in my current position and through my church involvement.

I want to reiterate my strong interest in working with you and the Orlando YMCA. Please keep in mind my personal attraction to this work that goes beyond just my academic credentials. I trust this gives me an added component as an appropriate candidate.

Again, thank you for considering me for this opportunity to build positive characteristics in the lives of young people and the chance to serve our community. As we discussed, I will call you Thursday morning to check the status of your decision.

Sincerely,

Charles S. Miller

Notice the strong "selling" language still being presented. Don't be afraid to tell them you want the position and that you think you are the best candidate. If you aren't convinced of that, it will be difficult for the interviewer to believe it.

PERSONAL MISSION STATEMENT WORKSHEET

Drawing from the information you have already completed, fill in this simple worksheet. Look at the examples on the next page and just get something down for yourself. You can come back to it and refine it over time, but there is real power in having something to help you focus what your life is really all about. Remember: If you can get something down on paper, it will separate you from about 98 percent of the people on earth.

This is only a summary of the components you have been developing throughout this book. Write them down and integrate them into your own Personal Mission Statement. (See examples on the next page.)

Skills and interests:

_____

_____

_____

Personality traits:

_____

_____

_____

Values, dreams, and passions:

_____

_____

_____

MY MISSION IS:

_____

_____

_____

_____

_____

"Based on the gift they have received, everyone should use it to serve others, as good managers of the varied grace of God."

1 Peter 4:10

SAMPLE MISSION STATEMENTS

I will maintain a positive attitude and sense of humor in everything I do. I want to be known by my family as a caring and loving husband and father, by my business associates as a fair and honest person, and by my friends as someone they can count on. To the people who work for me and with me, I pledge my respect, and I will strive every day to earn their respect. Controlling all my actions is a strong sense of integrity that I believe to be my most important character trait.

❖

My mission is to provide service, products, and benefits with integrity and honesty to the medical community. I will look for opportunities to help hurting individuals and assist other professionals in a win-win manner. I will not knowingly harm or take advantage of anyone. I will use my knowledge and abilities in organizing and structuring in ways that provide income and pleasure for my family and blessings to those around me.

❖

My mission is to exercise my creativity and innovative ideas by developing songs, books, and products that change lives and society for the better. I will use my talents and abilities consistently. I will not hide them simply because they will not always be immediately recognized. I want all of my work to be a product of God's inspiration and a blessing to the world. I will be loyal to family, friends, and God.

❖

My mission is to use my skills and experience in design to help people realize their dreams for their homes and themselves. To do this with increasing effectiveness, I will study and expand my own knowledge in God's Word, design, finance, sales, and social skills. I will strive for loving relationships with my immediate and extended family and many friends. I will invest love, service, time, patience, encouragement, and creativity into those relationships. I will listen more than I talk and be transparent in sharing personal insights and struggles. From now on I will strive for excellence in all of the above and in my hobby of music.

Suggested Reading List

Books

Allen, Robert G. *Multiple Streams of Income.* A masterful guide to insulating yourself against corporate decisions by developing multiple streams of income.

Bolles, Richard Nelson. *What Color Is Your Parachute?* The best single source for the career process. Updated every year, the book has many practical tips and processes for guiding you through the search.

———. *Where Do I Go from Here with My Life?* A very practical and effective life/work planning manual for all ages.

Boldt, Laurence G. *Zen and the Art of Making a Living.* Another artistic way to look at the life you want and then develop your career around that.

Buford, Bob. *Halftime.* This book takes a Christian look at the change in life where we become more interested in significance than success.

Cameron, Julia. *The Artist's Way.* A delightful guide to rediscovering your creativity and authentic self.

Carnegie, Dale. *How to Stop Worrying and Start Living.* Based on the premise, "What's the worst that could happen?" this book teaches you to build from there. If you've had a disaster in your life, this book can encourage you to look at where you are and move forward.

———. *How to Win Friends and Influence People.* Old-time favorite about how to treat people and gain positive influence.

Covey, Stephen R. *The 7 Habits of Highly Effective People.* Dynamic presentation of how to develop direction and a personal mission statement. It's rather textbookish, but don't get bogged down in the details; just understand the principles.

———. *First Things First.* Expanding on the *7 Habits,* shows how to set clear priorities in your life.

Edwards, Paul and Sarah. *Making It on Your Own.* How to change your thinking from employee to working for yourself. In today's work environment, you need to be willing to look at new work models.

————. *Working From Home.* Everything you need to know about living and working under the same roof.

Eikleberry, Carol. *The Career Guide for Creative and Unconventional People.* A wonderful guide for applying your artistic, writing, musical, or other creative skills in ways that can make you money.

Frankl, Viktor E. *Man's Search for Meaning.* A classic work by a concentration camp prisoner, who shows that even when everything else is taken away, we have the ability to choose. (I read this about every 6 months just to remind myself of what is really important.)

Guinness, Os. *The Call.* A critical-thinking book about how to find God's central purpose for our lives.

Hansen, Mark Victor and Robert G. Allen. *The One Minute Millionaire.* Presenting the enlightened way to wealth—not at the expense of but by helping others in the process. A must-read.

Hill, Napoleon. *Think and Grow Rich.* One of the greatest best-sellers of all time about how to think yourself into a new way of living.

Johnson, Spencer. *Who Moved My Cheese?* A modern allegory about changing work environments. Don't expect things to always be the same. If you are not prepared, you will feel like a victim.

Jones, Laurie Beth. *The Path.* A great resource for creating your mission statement for work and for life. Whereas *7 Habits of Highly Successful People* will tell you the importance of a mission statement, *The Path* will show you how to do it.

Lee, Blaine. *The Power Principle.* Another great book from Covey Leadership Center. Living by the book's principles will do more for your true success than having a marketing strategy for a new product.

Levinson, Jay Conrad. *The Guerrilla Marketing Handbook.* Great tips for marketing yourself or your small business. Jay has several books on guerilla marketing that are all very useful and practical for low-cost ways to build your business.

Pink, Daniel. *Free Agent Nation.* Does a great job of describing the changing model of "employee" to "free agent."

Ramsey, Dave. *Financial Peace.* The best all-around source for getting your finances in order. This *New York Times* best-seller has transformed the finances of thousands.

Robbins, Alexandra and Abby Wilner. *Quarterlife Crisis*. Yes, they really do go through the challenges of people in their 20s: the disappointments, broken dreams, unfulfilled relationships, etc.

Schwartz, David J. *The Magic of Thinking Big*. Workable methods for thinking big. How to create your own "good luck." The book that put coach Lou Holtz on the road to extraordinary success.

Shenson, Howard. *Shenson on Consulting*. The best overview of making the transition from a regular job to consulting.

Sinetar, Marsha. *To Build the Life You Want, Create the Work You Love*. An excellent guide to looking at your life and building priorities around your values. Marsha is a delightful writer who will challenge your thinking and convince you that doing what you love is possible.

Stanley, Thomas J. *The Millionaire Mind*. A phenomenal follow-up to *The Millionaire Next Door*. This one tells the top common characteristics of truly wealthy people. They might surprise you.

———. *The Millionaire Next Door*. An excellent overview of wealth-building principles.

U.S. Department of Labor Dictionary of Occupational Titles. Descriptions of many jobs and vocations accessed online at www.oalj.dol.gov/libdot.htm.

Weiss, Andrew. *Million Dollar Consulting*. A textbook manual on becoming a high-level consultant.

Zelinski, Ernie J. *The Joy of Not Working*. A humorous look at the benefits of not working.

Ziglar, Zig. *See You at the Top*. Long-time favorite about positive thinking and winning attitudes. One of my personal favorites for children, teenagers, and adults.

Audio Tapes and CDs*

Tapes and CDs are a powerful method of absorbing new information and increasing your ability to go to new levels of accomplishment. If you travel 25,000 miles in your car each year at an average speed of 46 mph, you will spend approximately the same amount of time in your car as a college student does in an average year of class work. The question is, What will you do with that time? Will you spend it by listening to meaningless input or by yelling at the driver next to you, or will you invest it in something that can dramatically change the results you are getting in life? These tapes can propel you to the success you are seeking. Don't try to learn the lessons of life slowly; learn from the masters who are willing to pass on the wisdom of the ages quickly.

Abraham, Jay. *Your Secret Wealth.* Jay is an incredible thinker and innovator. He is a master at showing people how to use leverage and optimization to multiply their income.

Hill, Napoleon. *The Science of Personal Achievement.* A wonderful collection of original speeches given by the author of *Think and Grow Rich.*

Kiyosaki, Robert. *Rich Dad Secrets.* Secrets to money, business, and investing . . . and how you can profit from them.

Nightingale, Earl. *Lead the Field.* An old classic used by thousands of salespeople.

Templeton, Sir John. *Laws of Inner Wealth.* Principles for spiritual and material abundance.

Tracy, Brian. *Getting Rich in America.* The best information I have found on starting your own business.

———. *The Psychology of Selling.* The best compact training course in selling skills and techniques I have been able to find.

———. *The Universal Laws of Success and Achievement.* Tracy does a great job of overviewing the principles for success, happiness, and achievement.

Waitley, Denis. *The Psychology of Winning.* One of the best-selling tape sets of all time. Used to train Olympic athletes.

* Most of these tape sets are available from Nightingale-Conant at 1-800-323-5552 or www.nightingale.com. Call for a free catalogue of sales and motivational tapes.

HELPFUL INTERNET SITES FOR JOB-HUNTING

If you have been on this planet during the last few years, you know that the Internet provides a nearly unlimited amount of information on any subject. Careers are certainly no exception. You can research companies, post your résumé, review current job openings, explore your own business opportunities, and plan your financial retirement all on the Internet.

You may be thinking, *How can all this information be of value if it is free?* Well, trust me, you will be exposed to a variety of advertising as you make your way around the Internet. However, the job-hunting information you will find is very valuable and can save you an immense amount of time in preparing and planning your course of action.

Note of caution: While the Internet is a very helpful source of information, I do not recommend it as a quick cure for everything you need. Posting a résumé there is somewhat like dropping a few of them out of an airplane. Looking for a job online has the same challenges as in the newspaper: what you see is also seen by thousands of other job seekers. As previously mentioned, 75 percent of companies that have hired over the Internet say they have had a bad experience. Hiring is still very much a nose-to-nose process. Use this to your advantage. Make personal contacts and find opportunities others won't find.

One other note: Internet addresses change with the wind. Even major organizations change sites quickly and often. If a link is not active, just move on. There are plenty to choose from.

Here are only a few of the sites I have found to be most helpful:

www.jobhuntersbible.com (This site has a constantly updated version of job-hunting on the Internet from *What Color Is Your Parachute?*)

www.careers.org (Lists over 11,000 links to jobs, employers, and business, education and career service professionals on the Web, plus 6,000 other helpful career resources.)

TOP JOB BOARDS

www.monster.com
www.careerbuilder.com
www.hotjobs.com

www.flipdog.com
www.jobsearch.org
www.net-temps.com
www.vault.com
www.4jobs.com
www.employment911.com
www.nationjob.com
www.job.com
www.employmentguide.com
www.careersite.com
www.directemployers.com
www.jobbankusa.com
www.topusajobs.com
www.wetfeet.com
www.coolworks.com
www.snagajob.com
www.careermag.com
www.truecareers.com
www.jobwarehouse.com
www.localcareers.com
www.preferredjobs.com
www.bestjobsusa.com
www.sologig.com
www.hiregate.com
www.jobfind.com
www.careershop.com
www.groovejob.com
www.summerjobs.com
www.employmentspot.com
www.americanjobs.com
www.4work.com

TOP JOB POSTINGS

www.ajb.dni.us—maintained by the Dept. of Labor, U.S. Employment Service (links 2,000 state employment service offices)

www.careerbuilder.com—features some 32,000 ads from eight major newspapers in the U.S.

www.monstertrak.com—lists over 2,100 new job postings each day, primarily for college students, graduates, and alumni.

www.monster.com—a megacollection of more than 50,000 job listings. This site also has a personal search agent called Swoop, which is free to job hunters.

www.careersonline.com.au/col/AskCOL.html—offers bilingual career aptitude testing, career design seminars, job search counseling, résumé preparation, and career counseling.

www.dice.com—a database for financial and technical careers.

www.jobbankusa.com—provides employment networking and information services to job seekers, employers, and recruitment firms.

www.cooljobs.com—"cool" positions listed here.

CAREER COUNSELING ONLINE

www.jobsmart.org

www.myemploymentlawyer.com—for help with a legal question.

www.bls.gov—see the latest U.S. government figures regarding employment trends and issues.

www.workforce.com—more on employee and legal issues.

SALARIES

www.salary.com—the best overall salary site, complete with relocation calculator and a very thorough list of career areas.

www.jobstar.org/tools/salary/index.htm—a pretty complete list of salaries on the Net.

www.stats.bls.gov/oco—find salary trends in the official "Occupational Outlook Handbook."

HELPFUL INTERNET SITES FOR SMALL BUSINESSES

www.workingsolo.com—lists 1,200 business resources for those seeking self-employment.

www.sbaonline.sba.gov—this U.S. Small Business Administration site has a massive amount of information and lots of links.

www.nfib.com—a wonderful site by the National Federation of Independent Business with daily information on legislation affecting small businesses and tips for being more successful.

www.entrepreneur.com—find a business for sale, business-building information, business opportunities, and more.

www.aahbb.org—the American Association of Home-Based Businesses.

www.madetoorderwebsites.com—for an inexpensive Web site to start your business.

www.nationalbusiness.org—National Business Association.

www.nmbc.org—the National Minority Business Council.

www.soho.org—Small Office Home Office helps home-office professionals.

HELPFUL INTERNET SITES FOR WOMEN

With the shift from a time and effort economy to a results-based economy, more women have discovered ways to leverage their abilities into corporate and entrepreneurial ventures. Want to network with other women? In addition to the organizations listed below, check with your local women's Chamber of Commerce and industry associations.

- National Association for Female Executives, (800) 927-6233, www.nafe.com
- National Association of Women Business Owners, (800) 556-2926, www.nawbo.org
- Women Business Enterprise National Council, (202) 872-5515, www.wbenc.org
- Women's Foodservice Forum, (312) 780-7374, www.womensfoodserviceforum.com

COLLEGE-RELATED INTERNET SITES

Personal skills and passion are more important than traditional degrees. However, the options for getting formal degrees are becoming easier and more accessible. If you need additional training to pursue the work you love, here are some new options.

SCHOOLING OPTIONS:

www.classesusa.com—the most comprehensive site I know of for exploring distance-education options.

www.universityofphoenix.com—the University of Phoenix is the best-known and most rapidly growing alternative education option.

www.jec.edu—JEC College Connection works with 12 universities, offering a choice of 200 classes and 11 degree programs. Classes are taught primarily through videotapes and the Internet.

www.tesc.edu—Thomas Edison State College offers bachelor's degrees in 119 majors; 14 degree programs can be completed entirely through distance-learning.

www.lesko.com/help/EducationandTrainingHelp.htm—Matthew Lesko is a wild guy, but there is a ton of very helpful and interesting information here. You'll enjoy it!

FUNDING SCHOOLING OPTIONS

The National Commission on Student Financial Assistance reports that of the $7 billion dollars available in scholarships to students in 2002, only $400 million was claimed.

The thought of searching through thousands of books and manuals may be a daunting prospect; however, the Internet just made your search process much easier.

Without leaving the comfort of your own home, you can now access information on more than 300,000 different forms of scholarships in a matter of seconds.

You may have been approached about different companies or individuals that offer the search process for a fee, but you can do it on your own just as well. The reason so much power and service is offered for free is that while you are searching, you will be shown many friendly advertisements from vendors and suppliers who would like your business. In exchange for this promotional exposure, you will be given powerful up-to-the-minute searches to legitimately help you find money. Many of the sites will actually prepare request letters for you.

The following is a brief sampling of URL addresses that will be helpful in the scholarship search process.

www.fastweb.com—the Internet's largest free scholarship search. Will search daily for over 375,000 different awards.

www.finaid.org—find out how to estimate financial need, sources of financial aid, scholarships, grants, contests, tuition payment plans, and how to avoid scholarship scams.

www.fdncenter.org—the Foundation Center's site for philanthropy and giving to those in need. You might fall into an interesting category that some foundation wants to give to.

www.scholarshipseminar.homestead.com—a site managed and updated by my friend Mike Turner, an expert on the scholarship process.

www.ets.org—has standardized test information, practice questions, and college searches.

www.collegeboard.com—the College Board site for online SAT registration, test dates, and college searches.

www.gocollege.com—find college scholarship searches and practice for the SAT and ACT.

www.dir.yahoo.com/education/financial_aid—get access to college financial aid offices, sources of financial aid, grants, loans, and scholarship programs.

www.yahoo.com/education/higher_education—contains information about college and university academic competitions and honors programs.

www.fastaid.com

www.freschinfo.com

www.scholarsite.com

www.collegenet.com/mach25

This process does take time, but the results can provide a tremendous payback. Start at least 1 year in advance. The searches will go out each day and find new prospects for you. Then you must request the application forms and complete them.

The
48 Days Marketplace

48 DAYS TO THE WORK YOU LOVE®
WORKBOOK
BY DAN MILLER

This is the perfect companion to the book you now hold in your hands. This workbook is Dan's flagship product that came from more than a decade of business and life consulting and launched him into national awareness. The workbook and audio CD set is a hands-on, impacting tool that embodies the information and personal attention Dan gives his personal coaching clients. It has a ton of information that is updated continuously and is geared to help you clarify your specific personal desires, tendencies, and abilities and walk you through formulation of a plan of action that produces the results you want for your career life. The 126-page workbook comes with 2 audio CDs that go further toward Dan guiding you in making your dream vocation a reality.

48 Days to the Work You Love® Workbook & 2 Audio CDs
Available online at www.48days.com: $39.00

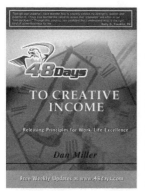

48 DAYS TO CREATIVE INCOME®
WORKBOOK
BY DAN MILLER

Do you have a desire to own your own business but haven't a clue how to get it off the ground? Are you wondering how you can generate extra income? Do you have an idea? A patent? An invention? Do you have a service to offer you feel sure would be successful? In this workbook and CD set, you will learn how to determine if you have the right personality to generate revenue with your own business idea, or what Dan has labeled an "Eaglepreneur."™ Also included is how to get started; how to best choose a product or service, sales, and marketing essentials; how to develop your idea or product; and much, much more. A *must* for anyone considering doing something nontraditional!

48 Days to Creative Income® *Workbook and 2 Audio CDs*
Available online at www.48days.com: $39.00

See the full line of Dan Miller's 48 Days Products:
• Career Tools • Articles
• Resources • Up-to-date Career News
and more @ www.48days.com